Other Works by Tim Barker

My Jesus Journey

My Jesus Journey: Crescendo

My Jesus Journey: Glissando

My Jesus Journey: Rhapsody

Our Privilege of Joy

God's Revelation and Your Future

Truth, Love & Redemption: The Holy Spirit for Today

The Vision of Nehemiah: God's Plan for Righteous Living

End Times

At Your Feet

NAMES
OF GOD

Thanks to ...

... my loving wife, Jill, for always
encouraging me in my ministry endeavors.
She is my motivation and inspiration.

NAMES OF GOD

Tim R. Barker, D. Min.

*Superintendent of the South Texas
District of the Assemblies of God*

Tim R. Barker Ministries

NAMES OF GOD, Barker, Tim.
1st ed.

Formatting, proofing, and cover provided by:
Farley Dunn
of
Three Skillet Publishing
●❋● THREE SKILLET
www.ThreeSkilletPublishing.com

Tim R. Barker Ministries

ISBN: 978-1-7346669-8-4

Dedication

Willard Fugate is one of the godliest men I know. God placed Willard in my life in the summer of 1998. He served as a member of the church board of McAllen First Assembly and was the chairman of the pulpit search committee. Little did I know when I connected with Willard that he would become a cherished friend and confidant. He & his sweet wife, Lenora, were "bad" influences when I first moved to the Valley when they introduced me to Tico's Botana platters (which are delicious, by the way). Willard and I share a love for Gospel music that elevates our souls and spirits. No one can lead the old hymns with more enthusiasm and zeal than Willard can. Even though we are now separated by miles, he in

Colorado and me in Texas, I know that my friend prays for me.

God has placed hundreds, perhaps thousands of special people in my life throughout my years of ministry, but Willard & Lenora Fugate are among those at the top of the list.

Table of Contents

Introduction

What's in a name?

Everything, of course. Our name gives us connectivity with the world around us. We use it to get people's attention, and as importantly, they use it to get ours.

Our name also tells people who we are. In past centuries, a youth might be called Jacobsen, or "Jacob's Son." Everyone knew just who he was.

Other names carry information about where we're from. Björk could only come from Iceland. Sankaran suggests India, and the surname O'Donnell is more than likely from the northern part of the British Isles.

What about the name Christian? That's what the followers of Jesus call themselves. What information can people glean about us when we put a fish symbol on the bumper of our car, or we wear a cross around our neck? And, importantly, do our actions live up to their expectations?

God is known as the Faithful One, as Absolute Truth, as Justice, Love, and Holiness.

We name Him Father, with all the meanings that imbues Him with. Shaddai, Rapha, Nissi. Who is God to you?

He wants to be all of these, and He can be, if you invite Him to be Lord of your life and the Master of your heart. He WILL live up to each one.

When you finish this book, the Name of God will be clearer to you than ever before. And you will learn His name for you as you turn the pages of this book.

You are a Child of the Everlasting King.

— I —

IMMANUEL

God with Us!

one of the darkest moments of Judah's life as a kingdom, God proclaimed one of the brightest promises ... provided they walked in obedience with His plans and His Word. There may be times in your life when you find yourself closed in on all fronts by the enemy ... what

do you do when this happens? For some people, fear causes them to do nothing ... which leaves them frozen in inaction and ripe for the enemy.

The usual reactions of most are frustration, doubt, fear, anxiety ... the sense of confinement. If the dark situation is NOT THE RESULT of our disobedience to God's Word, we can have hope, and even if it is because of disobedience to God's Word and we are willing to repent, God can bring us hope again ... for He made a promise to Judah that still is the greatest promise to mankind today ... THE PROMISE THAT GOD WILL BE WITH US!

One of the greatest prophecies about Jesus coming into the world as a babe was the name He would have: IMMANUEL, which translated means: "God with us!" So, if darkness surrounds us, either innocently or even because of disobedience; and if we repent and submit to God, HE promises to be with us!

STANDING IN FEAR!

Normal Reactions:

Isaiah 7:2 ~

Now the house of David was told, "Aram has allied itself with Ephraim"; so the hearts of Ahaz and his people were shaken, as the trees of the forest are shaken by the wind.

Ahaz and Judah's situation was bad.

Judah was the Southern Kingdom in Israel, and the Northern Kingdom, their own Jewish brothers, were planning their demise! (With some foreign help, of course.) In a sense, Judah had brought some of this upon themselves; they had been living in disobedience to God and His Word, thus they had exposed themselves to evil influences.

Their reactions were much like ours when we find ourselves surrounded: Fear gripped the king and the nation! What were they to do?

Isaiah 7:2b ~

... so the hearts of Ahaz and his people were shaken, as the trees of the forest are shaken by the wind.

They felt overwhelmed ... who could possibly help them; the problem was greater than their strength and resources! They had a real problem on their hands ... yet God was allowing such a situation to turn them from their disobedience. Their next step would be crucial. Would they turn back to God or would they try to solve it their own way with their own strength? This is always the consummate question when we hit these places in our lives — and it can get us deeper into trouble when we try and solve it in our own wisdom and strength!

The quality of the outcome would be determined by what they chose! All they could see at the moment was FEAR ... and lots of it too!

Needed Revelation!

Isaiah 7:3 ~

Then the Lord said to Isaiah, "Go out, you and your son Shear-Jashub, to meet Ahaz at the end of the aqueduct of the Upper Pool, on the road to the Launderer's Field."

Isaiah 9:6 ~

For to us a child is born, to us a son is given, and the government will be on his shoulders. And he will be called Wonderful Counselor, Mighty God, Everlasting Father, Prince of Peace.

First, they needed to understand God's purpose in this situation ... to wake them up to their need to repent and trust God! What they needed was what Isaiah 7:3 begins with: "THEN THE LORD SAID ..." This was their problem. Until then it had been what they said, not what God said! If we listen, God has an answer for us!

Part of the answer was confronting the king with God's answer, not just personal opinions. The ultimate revelation would be found in the prophecy of Isaiah 9:6. "A CHILD IS BORN" – Christ's humanity! He would experience our life and hurts. He would know birth, growth, hunger, thirst, exhaustion, disappointment, pain, a troubled heart, tears and even physical death! Does God really understand us, and can He really identify with us in our humanity? Too often we have viewed Jesus as floating around on this earth for three years doing miracles and having a glowing halo over Him ... speaking parables every time He spoke ... always under control and confident of His mission; but the Scriptures portray for us His identification with humanity as well, and for a good reason!

HUMANITY OF CHRIST

Hebrews 2:17 ~

For this reason he had to be made like them, fully human in every way, in order that he might become a merciful and faithful high priest in service to God, and that he might make atonement for the sins of the people.

Hebrews 4:15 ~

For we do not have a high priest who is unable to

empathize with our weaknesses, but we have one who has been tempted in every way, just as we are—yet he did not sin.

John 1:14 ~

The Word became flesh and made his dwelling among us. We have seen his glory, the glory of the one and only Son, who came from the Father, full of grace and truth.

In every way, Jesus experienced life on the earth the same way we do:

~ Birth
~ Growth – as a youth and teen
~ Hungered and ate
~ Thirsted and Drank
~ Had parents and brothers
~ Knew loneliness
~ Became weary
~ Was troubled in Spirit
~ Wept
~ Slept
~ Was surprised
~ Had financial pressures, taxes, and treasury
~ Got angry

~ Knew physical pain
~ Had to be taught – learned
~ Taught others
~ Did household chores
~ Held down a job at one time – was an employee
~ Learned to cook
~ Settled arguments
~ Went to church (the synagogue)
~ Had to be obedient to others over Him
~ Had to make hard decisions (Gethsemane)
~ Knew what it was to be misunderstood by others
~ Experienced the feeling God had forsaken Him
~ Even experienced death
~ Knew the feeling of losing a friend (Lazarus)
~ Knew the feeling of failure (Judas)
~ Knew the emotions of joy and happiness (wedding celebration)
~ Needed friends
~ Knew what it was to be treated unfairly
~ Knew what it was to need to be reassured ("THIS IS MY BELOVED SON IN WHOM I AM WELL PLEASED.")
~ Knew what it was to give love (little children, disciples, lost sinners)
~ Knew what it was to be tempted to disobey God's Word
~ Learned obedience to others and submission to

authority (parents and nation)

~ Experienced the need to help others as well (healing, feeding, etc.)

~ Learned what it was to need to pray and spend time with God!

WHAT KINDS OF THINGS DO YOU THINK JESUS WOULD HAVE DONE HAD HE LIVED TODAY? Would He eat at McDonalds? Whataburger, I'm certain! Hold down a job at Walmart? Would He drive a Ford or Chevrolet? Visit malls? Shop on Amazon? God came as a human as well as divine and lived among us! This hardly looks like an answer at first! Ahaz would have thought the same thing … "What we need is an army, not a baby!" was probably in his mind! God's way of solving the most difficult problem of humanity was found in a manger, of all places — really! God still baffles the mind in how He solves our most difficult problems; many times His solutions are so different from what we would have thought!

"A SON IS GIVEN" – CHRIST'S DEITY

The Son could not be born since He has always been the Son, but He could be given … to you and me! What a solution; to give us — you and me, the most powerful source in the universe. How could anything outdo this?

Yet, even in this there is a condition. You must accept the gift or you don't possess it! How many have missed the greatest gift of God because of the fear of the unknown? And so, with Judah and King Ahaz ... God promised them victory, but with a condition.

Necessary Reassurance:

Isaiah 7:4 ~

Be careful, keep calm, and don't be afraid ...

God tells him to stay calm BEFORE He tells him the answer to the problem! The point: GOD STARTS WITH US, NOT ALWAYS WITH THE PROBLEM FIRST! ... SOMETIMES WE ARE THE PROBLEM! Isaiah begins to reassure Ahaz, an important ministry! We need in the church people who are builders of faith! This was not just wishful thinking on Isaiah's part ... although Isaiah would tell Ahaz that he must exercise faith in order for God to solve the problem! Barnabus in the New Testament serves as a good example of this. His name literally meant: "SON OF CONSOLATION (encouragement)!" This doesn't mean that Barnabus ignored sin in other people's lives, just that he encouraged them to trust God and to repent! Us, too, we must encourage one another, but not to the extent we ignore sin, our own sin or sin in others! IN LIGHT OF GOD'S PROMISE TO BE "IMMAN-UEL" (or "God with us") these two kings who were going to come against them were in God's eyes nothing but two smoldering twigs! (Isa. 7:4) Though the world doesn't take God seriously, we must! The world only sees Christ as an "ornament" in our culture ... but we must be careful to see Him as the ALL-SUFFICIENT ONE.

It's been said that society never actually wanted the Incarnation. "Immanuel, God-with-Us" does not sell computer games or cologne. Society wants the cute stuff — rustic stable, adoring shepherds, fluffy sheep, cows, donkey, holy family, infant Jesus, gift-bearing kings, stars, angels, St. Nicholas, reindeer, fir trees, holly, and presents. The pagan stuff they will retain — even if they do dye the trees powder blue and decorate them with miniature hanging appliances and Disney ornaments ...

The marketplace will also retain some of the traditional hymnody, but in upbeat arrangements that remove them from the realm of traditional worship. Ancient chants are popular, too. They sound religious and profound and — best of all — nobody understands Latin, so no shoppers are offended

And so, it is with us in our most pressing problems ... they are no match for God if we follow His ways. We don't have to be overcome by circumstances but can be overcomers!

STANDING IN FAITH!

Never Retreat!

Isaiah 7:10-13 ~

[10]Again the Lord spoke to Ahaz, [11]"Ask the Lord your God for a sign, whether in the deepest depths or in the highest heights." [12]But Ahaz said, "I will not ask; I will not put the Lord to the test." [13]Then Isaiah said, "Hear now, you house of David! Is it not enough to try the patience of humans? Will you try the patience of my God also?"

God always has a plan ... we just need to FIND and FOLLOW it! Here is where Ahaz blew it! Isaiah reveals God's plan ... and calls upon Ahaz to have faith! Ahaz has a choice ... so did all Judah ... so do we! The one word jumps out of verse 9: "IF."

God will bring victory, but we must stand repentant and faithful. Ahaz tried to sound spiritual in his rejection of God's offer of help. In this passage, what he was really saying in a very spiritual-sounding way was: "I WON'T OBEY YOU, GOD!" It is bad enough not to trust close friends, but not to trust God is really bad! A friend may fail you ... but God cannot! He is trustworthy! Not trusting God is like trying His patience! Those in this world hardly take it seriously! Even some in the religious world ignore the power of the reality of Christ's coming. "God with us!" The religious leaders of Jesus' day certainly didn't take Him seriously! How about us?

What's Your Excuse When God Speaks?

~ "I want to be a good steward of God's money by not using too much gas to go to church too often." (When the real issue is a failure to tithe.)

~ "Since God wants me to love people I try and never mention sin in any way so as not to offend anyone." (When the real issue is avoiding dealing with sin.)

~ "The Bible teaches moderation in all things, so I try not to go to church too much or talk too much about salvation." (When the real issue is lack of commitment.)

~ "I know the Lord wants me to be a good example and witness in paying my bills, so when we get caught up we will begin to tithe!" (When the real issue is stewardship.)

~ "The Bible says God loves the 'cheerful giver,' so once my attitude is right we will begin to give." (When the real issue is lack of giving.)

These excuses and others are only retreats from

God's plans and His divine will; they may sound spiritual ... but they are only cop-outs! Disobedience can have serious consequences.

Captivity and pain resulted from Ahaz and Judah's failure to obey and repent! There was a real price tag for sin!

Now Revealed!

The promise of God to help them!

Isaiah 7:14 ~

Therefore the Lord himself will give you a sign: The virgin will conceive and give birth to a son, and will call him Immanuel.

IMMANUEL – "God with us!" What else could they hope for ... if God is for you, who can be against you? Ahaz and Judah missed the hope they could have had ... another generation had the privilege of seeing "IMMANUEL" because this generation failed the "IF" test. Repentance and obedience could have brought a different experience for them. It doesn't get any better than having "GOD WITH YOU!" This is the Christmas story ... "GOD WITH US." Our faith doesn't have to be huge to start with; even having small faith to begin with will help, and it will grow as we exercise it. God came as a small baby; we must start somewhere, even if small!

Faith doesn't have to be huge ... just use what you have at first. For example: the bridge over Niagara Falls started by a piece of string, ending in a suspension bridge! First, a kite with a string was flown over the river, then a cord was attached to it and pulled over, then a light rope was pulled over, then a heavy rope, then a piece of wire thicker than the rope, and finally the steel suspension system was in place to support the rest of the structure ... begin with what faith you have and let God build it little by little! – Source Unknown

Faith grows in time and practice. In Matthew 1:22-23 this promise unfolds:

Matthew 1:22-23 ~

22All this took place to fulfill what the Lord had said through the prophet: 23"The virgin will conceive and give birth to a son, and they will call him Immanuel" (which means "God with us").

Though again, the promise comes with a condition, that we believe on the Son and repent of our sins: the same conditions given to Judah! What problem could possibly overshadow this provision! NONE! "IMMAN-UEL" – "God with us!" When the enemy had a plan ... God had one too – His name was JESUS! While the WORLD WAITS IN FEAR, the BELIEVER CAN WAIT IN FAITH! The choice, though, is still ours to make! The bottom line: "IF YOU DON'T STAND FIRM IN YOUR FAITH, YOU WILL NOT STAND AT ALL!" (Isa. 7:9b) FAITH-FUL not FEAR-FUL!

The greatest revelation of Christ's birth is that He is "IMMANUEL" meaning "GOD WITH US." If He is for us – and He is with us, who can be against us? NO ONE or NO THING! The only reason to fear is if we haven't repented or we aren't trusting God ... stand in forgiveness and faith and you can't lose ... GOD WILL BE WITH YOU!

JEHOVAH-OLAM

The Everlasting God!

brand of vacuum cleaners recently on TV portrayed their product as lasting well into the 21st century ... practically everlasting!

We have long-lasting nasal sprays ... their selling point is that they last longer than brand X ... they almost last forever! (Almost?)

Midas claims their mufflers will last almost indefinitely; they are almost everlasting! (As long as you own the car and it is still running, that is.)

There's more: steel belted radials, alkaline batteries — everything lasts "longer" these days!

We can't even conceive of "everlasting" ... and even if we could, we would likely try and find a way to misuse it!

I heard of a man who asked God how long a million years was to Him. God replied, "It's just like a single second of your time, my child." So, the man asked, "And what about a million dollars?" The Lord replied, "To me, it's just like a single penny." So the man gathered himself up and said, "Well, Lord, could I have one of your pennies?" And God said, "Certainly, my child, just a second."

For all the products man has made, none has yet proven to have achieved the goal of being "everlasting!" In fact, not even creation itself will be as we now know it! The Scriptures teach us that we serve an everlasting God; we have our security and our eternal life because He is the Everlasting God!

HIS PERSON IS EVERLASTING!

Reliable:

Psalm 90:1 ~

*Lord, you have been our dwelling place throughout
all generations.*

"Throughout all generations." God is our "dwelling
place" in the past. He is our "dwelling place" in the
present. We can trust Him to be our "dwelling place" in
the future.

God has clearly created in mankind the sense of
"eternity." Hence our need to experience Him.

Bill Hybels in one of his books mentions that if you
ever get the opportunity to visit Egypt and the tombs
and pyramids, study what was required to construct
some of those monuments. Some studies revealed that it
required the efforts of one hundred thousand workers
for forty years to build one of the great pyramids. As you
tour the area there, you can't help but ask why. Why so
much effort? Why would somebody put that amount of
emphasis on a tomb, on the afterlife?

The answer is that the Egyptians understood full
well they would spend a lot more time in the afterlife
than they would spend in this life. Granted, some of
their conceptions of what would happen in the afterlife
were a little skewed. But the point is, they understood to
the core of their being that the afterlife was a whole lot

more important than this life, and so they prepared for the afterlife during this life. God had placed eternity in their hearts.

Refuge:

God is reliable – you can count on Him! Not just now ... but forever! This prayer of Moses, found in this Psalm, establishes the fact of God's reliability: *"... our dwelling place throughout all generations."*

A place of safety – "dwelling place." Our peace and security are found in God, not goods! Since this was Moses' prayer, if anyone knew how important a "dwelling place" was in the desert, Moses would ... and he was clear that God was their dwelling place, not the desert! *"Lord, you have been our dwelling place ..."* Our rest is in God, not property or material things.

Hebrews 4:3 ~

Now we who have believed enter that rest, just as God has said, "So I declared on oath in my anger, 'They shall never enter my rest.'"

And yet His works have been finished since the creation of the world. This rest is a never-ending one, a Sabbath principle! There is nothing else in this world that seems to satisfy the human soul, nothing material, or man would never have sought out God.

C.S. Lewis once said, "If I find in myself a desire which no experience in this world can satisfy, the most probable explanation is that I was made for another world."

We have a place of protection. Satan can't tread on us – we are hidden in Christ! We are Christ's; Satan has no power or claim on us!

Ruling:

Psalm 90:2 ~

Before the mountains were born or you brought forth the whole world, from everlasting to everlasting you are God.

God rules creation and over His creatures! His being is eternal. *"Before the mountains were born or you brought forth the earth and the world, from everlasting to everlasting you are God."* God is hard to comprehend because we have not physically seen Him except in Christ. This sometimes is the reason I think so many struggle over God. But, this still doesn't change His essential character: He is Eternal or Everlasting!

He never changes or wears out. *"They will perish,*

but you remain; they will all wear out like a garment. Like clothing you will change them and they will be discarded. But you remain the same, and your years will never end." (Psa. 102:26-27) He is the one constant in existence, He is over all! *"For a thousand years in your sight are like a day that has just gone by, or like a watch in the night."* (Psa. 90:4)

HIS PRECEPTS ARE EVERLASTING!

God doesn't change His ideas of righteousness — what was sin thousands of years ago is still sin today, and will be sin a hundred years from now if Christ doesn't come until then! God is not capricious. God is not reticent, either; He has spoken! The problem is that man is recalcitrant in nature! "He's as good as His word!" That is true of God! That is true of His Word, too! God and His Word are everlasting!

In Greek mythology, Aurora, the goddess of the dawn, fell in love with Tithonus, a mortal youth. Zeus, the king of the gods, gave her the privilege of choosing a gift for her mortal lover. Aurora asked that Tithonus live forever; however, she forgot to ask that Tithonus remain forever young; consequently, Tithonus grew progressively older; in fact, he could never die. The gift became a curse. The God of the Bible is not like a mythological god. He never forgets anything that is not considered before He answers our prayers. He does not grant us a request which ultimately will become a burden. He is never a deceiver. Therefore, we must accept His answers as the best for us. — Source Unknown

Those who try and change God's standards are trying to change God! God's call to righteous living will not change for His people; it is everlasting because His Word is! We must not try and explain it away. We must not water it down. We must not try and update it. Our call is to obey it! *"Therefore, prepare your minds for action; be self-controlled;"* (I Pet. I:13a)

Renewing:

I Peter I:22-25 ~

²²Now that you have purified yourselves by obeying the truth so that you have sincere love for each other, love one another deeply, from the heart. ²³For you have been born again, not of perishable seed, but of imperishable, through the living and enduring word of God. ²⁴For, "All people are like grass, and all their glory is like the flowers of the field; the grass withers and the flowers fall, *25but the word of the Lord endures forever." And this is the word that was preached to you.*

His Word renews us who have faith in Him. His Word damns those who do not have faith in Him. This renewal for His people enables us to love deeply – from our hearts. Our birth and renewal are ongoing ... there will be growth continuing. God's precepts will continue to bring His people renewal! God's principles never wear out; some stuff in this world claims to never wear out, but that is just hyperbole.

God's love is powerful, but even the offer of salvation has a "time frame" ... this lifetime only. We need to take advantage of it while we can.

Receiving:

I Peter 2:1-3 ~

1Therefore, rid yourselves of all malice and all deceit, hypocrisy, envy, and slander of every kind. 2Like newborn babies, crave pure spiritual milk, so that by it you may grow upon your salvation, 3now that you have tasted that the Lord is good.

We must receive God's Word as a baby does milk. It is our source of growth and strength. We desire it like a baby does milk without doubting its contents! In it we receive energy for living! It will make us mature if we receive it, sickly if we ignore it! Many Christians have stunted growth because they are not receiving God's Word.

I remember reading about a U.S. soldier in 1958 that wandered the streets of Berlin to see the sights. Despite the bustling new life in parts of the city, reminders remained of the destruction of World War II. Walking through a residential area one evening, across the cobble-stone street he saw an open space edged with flowers. In the center stood the stone front of what had been a church. The building was no longer there, but the rubble had been cleared away in an attempt to fill the empty space with a little park. The former church's main door was shaped in a Gothic arch, and over it was carved into the stone in German: HEAVEN AND EARTH WILL PASS AWAY BUT MY WORDS WILL NOT PASS AWAY. As he stepped through the arch where the doors had once been, of course he wasn't inside anything. What was once a place of worship had been reduced to a patch of stone pavement and open sky. Not so with the Door — Jesus Christ! As we step into Christ, we enter into His unshakable, eternal presence. It cannot be reduced; it can only be experienced — forever.

God's Word will not pass away; we need it in this life to prepare for the next. Without it we are spiritually malnourished! God's Word builds strong bodies!

HIS PATIENCE IS EVERLASTING!

Jeremiah 3:3-6 ~

³*"Therefore the showers have been withheld, and no spring rains have fallen. Yet you have the brazen look of a prostitute; you refuse to blush with shame.* ⁴*Have you not just called to me: 'My Father, my friend from my youth,* ⁵*will you always be angry? Will your wrath continue forever?' This is how you talk, but you do all the evil you can."* ⁶*During the reign of King Josiah, the Lord said to me, "Have you seen what faithless Israel has done? She has gone up on every high hill and under every spreading tree and has committed adultery there."*

RESTORING – AN EVERLASTING LOVE

Jeremiah 31:3 ~

The LORD appeared to us in the past, saying: "I have loved you with an everlasting love; I have drawn you with loving-kindness."

Love is patient and kind. God allows time for our growth.

Jeremiah 31:4 ~

"I will build you up again and you will be rebuilt, O Virgin Israel."

Babies don't grow up overnight. Patience restores us to God's favor so God can work in and through us! This verse goes on to say, *"Again, you will take up your tambourines and go out to dance with the joyful."* God is working in us and through us.

There is a legend told of an ancient kingdom whose sovereign had just died, and whose ambassadors were sent to choose a successor from twin infants. They found the little fellows fast asleep, and looking at them carefully, agreed that it was difficult to decide, until they happened to notice one curious small difference between them. As they lay, one infant had his tiny fists closed tight; the other slept with his little hands wide open. Instantly, they made their selection of the latter. The legend very properly concludes with the record that, as he grew up in his station, he came to be known as the King with the Open Hand. We could say the same thing of our God. His hand is always open to give. — Source Unknown

He doesn't give up on us, even when others do! His love is everlasting. And His love comes with an "Open Hand" ... He died and rose again to grant us His grace. God allows for growth to take place over time. He will build us up! *"I will build you up again and you will be rebuilt ... "* (Jer. 31:4)

We can rejoice because His patience is everlasting. He gave the Amorites and Canaanites and the other wicked tribes in the land of Canaan over 400 years to repent of their sin and wickedness before they were destroyed. God said this to Abraham many years earlier:

Genesis 15:16 ~

In the fourth generation your descendants will come back here, for the sin of the Amorites has not yet reached its full measure.

The Apostle Paul affirmed this also in rounding off the years to 400 in the following passage:

Acts 7:6-7 ~

God spoke to him in this way: "Your descendants will be strangers in a country not their own, and they will be enslaved and mistreated four hundred years. But I will punish the nation they serve as slaves," God said, "and afterward they will come out of that country and worship me in this place."

Part of the reason Israel was not set free in Egypt was to allow the full time of opportunity for all the distant "-ites" (Amorites, Canaanites, Perizzites, Hittites, Hivites and Jebusites, etc.) in the Promised Land the opportunity to repent, until the measure of their cup was full. It was actually nearly 430 years before God acted against those wicked nations — God gave a large window of grace to them. God is longsuffering in grace and gives great opportunity for repentance, but a day does come for judgment. We will rejoice in our God, who loves us with an everlasting love.

Martin Luther once was so depressed over a prolonged period that one day his wife came downstairs wearing all black. Martin Luther said, "Who died?" She said, "God has." He said, "God hasn't died." And she said, "Well, live like it and act like it." We should not act like God isn't real or everlasting! God as an everlasting God impacts our life NOW and FOREVER! This reality should reflect in our actions today, as well as tomorrow. We can celebrate — God is an everlasting God! There is hope for today, and for tomorrow!

Jude 24-25 ~

To Him who is able to keep you from falling and to present you before his glorious presence without fault and with great joy — to the only God our Savior be glory, majesty, power and authority, through Jesus Christ our Lord, before all ages, now and forevermore! AMEN!

— 3 —

JEHOVAH-SHALOM

The Lord Is Peace!

is restlessness in the world today — caused by many different problems. Governments are racing against time trying to solve problems in the hope they can bring peace to the world. Despite this, their efforts clearly fall short even when the appearances of peace are displayed outwardly!

We assume we would have peace if we had:

~ A decent salary a year per person
~ A nice home for every human being
~ No sickness or being ill
~ Plenty of food and water for everyone

If these things alone are the foundation of our peace, we will be frustrated constantly and never find peace! The Bible teaches us that our peace is found in God — not in goods; peace comes not from solving problems but from saving people! Then "the Lord is our Peace!" or Jehovah-Shalom!

PROBLEMS!

Judges 6:1-6 ~

¹ The Israelites did evil in the eyes of the Lord, and for seven years he gave them into the hands of the Midianites. ²Because the power of Midian was so oppressive, the Israelites prepared shelters for themselves in mountain clefts, caves and strongholds. ³Whenever the Israelites planted their crops, the Midianites, Amalekites and other eastern peoples invaded the country. ⁴They camped on the land and ruined the crops all the way to

Gaza and did not spare a living thing for Israel, neither sheep nor cattle nor donkeys. ⁵They came up with their livestock and their tents like swarms of locusts. It was impossible to count them or their camels; they invaded the land to ravage it. ⁶Midian so impoverished the Israelites that they cried out to the Lord for help.

POWER OF MIDIAN - FEELINGS OF HELPLESSNESS

This sounds like today. The enemy was greater than they were. Their failure to turn to God left them vulnerable, and they had to hide in fear. This was the result of sin. They knew they were on their own; their sins had separated them from God, giving them feelings of devastation and loneliness. Sin creates this sense of loneliness; we are outside of a relationship with God when we are living in sin.

They had taken measures in their own strength to protect themselves, and the results were inadequate, as they always are against a strong enemy. We have no control over life when we do it under our own power.

Planted & Ruined!

Their efforts never paid off. Whatever work they did was destroyed by others before they got the chance to enjoy the fruits of their labors. Their efforts were wasted. Others destroyed their hard work. They allowed themselves to become financially embarrassed. This, of course, left them broken and in poverty. No matter how hard they tried to get ahead, they fell behind.

Overwhelmed by Problems!

They tried to get ahead without God and instead only found misery. Their own strength was not enough to secure their present, much less their future.

They ignored their sins but hoped it didn't matter; it was the source of their lack of peace!

Lack of Food and Security:

God was not being cruel to them; He was allowing them to realize the fruit of going it alone and trusting in their own strength. The realization of the futility of making it on their own would drive them back to God.

Prayed for Help:

This is exactly what Israel needed. How beautiful that God was supplying their need! What was painful was also restoring them. We don't always see this side of pain, but this is why God many times allows pain into our lives.

No God, no peace; know God, know peace.

It got them praying again to the true God! These problems actually form the base that later will bring them true peace! Our peace is not found in what we have on this earth; it is found in what we are in Christ! They needed to learn that the Lord is their peace (Jehovah-Shalom), not their livelihood!

PRIORITIES!

Judges 6:7-9 ~

⁷When the Israelites cried out to the Lord because of Midian, ⁸he sent them a prophet, who said, "This is what the Lord, the God of Israel, says: I brought you up out of Egypt, out of the land of slavery. ⁹I rescued you from the hand of the Egyptians. And I delivered you from the hand of all your oppressors; I drove them out before you and gave you their land."

A prophet was sent to tell the world that, "What saith the Lord," is the foundation whereby we find peace; not, "What saith Merrill Lynch."

God sends them a prophet to send them His Word! This is the beginning of finding peace.

Ramsey MacDonald, one-time prime minister of

England, was discussing wi
official the possibility of last
expert on foreign affairs, was
minister's idealistic viewpoin
"The desire for peace does
MacDonald admitted, saying
does the desire for food satis
it gets you started toward a restaur......

If money is you
feel some p
If it is yo
and
bu

First, God reminds them of His deliverances in the past, so that they are inspired to believe for the present. God had delivered their ancestors, and He was able to do the same for them.

The road to peace is the road to God! The road to God is through Jesus Christ, the Word made flesh! God's Word will align our priorities, and when our lives line up to God's Word, peace results!

Priorities Secured!

Judges 6:10 ~

"I said to you, 'I am the Lord your God; do not worship the gods of the Amorites, in whose land you live.' But you have not listened to me."

God is first! When He is ... we are at peace! Whatever is first in your life will be the extent of your peace!

priority, then when you have it, you will
ace, and when you don't have it, you won't!
ur goods, then as long as they are in good shape
ou have them, you will feel some measure of peace,
when they break down or get lost, so does your
peace! All things of this world are temporary; therefore,
they can only offer you an external, temporary type of
peace! But God is Eternal and life with Him gives
Eternal peace that even begins in this life! Lack of peace
means lack of God!

In this confused world, some people have peace while
others go to pieces. God points this out to them, that
while He had delivered their forefathers, this new
generation had failed to follow God like their forefathers
had, and so they were drifting by themselves, helpless
victims of their enemies without God's help. That could
change, however, if they made the right decision to
wholeheartedly follow God again. They could hardly do
worse than they were at present; they were gaining
nothing at the moment!

PERSPECTIVE!

The presence of the Lord makes all the difference in
our circumstances.

Judges 6:11-13 ~

11 The angel of the Lord came and sat down under the oak in Ophrah that belonged to Joash the Abiezrite, where his son Gideon was threshing wheat in a winepress to keep it from the Midianites. 12 When the angel of the Lord appeared to Gideon, he said, "The Lord is with you, mighty warrior."

13 "Pardon me, my lord," Gideon replied, "but if the Lord is with us, why has all this happened to us? Where are all his wonders that our ancestors told us about when they said, 'Did not the Lord bring us up out of Egypt?' But now the Lord has abandoned us and given us into the hand of Midian."

Proper perspective is formed when we get together with God — in prayer and in His Word. It takes the Lord's presence to give us the Lord's perspective!

Billy Graham once said, "Peace is not arbitrary. It must be based upon definite facts. God has all the facts on His side; the world does not. Therefore, God, and not the world, can give peace."

God starts with a man ... He will begin His work with even one person willing to come to Him. Gideon is hardly the best candidate; in fact, he is the least of all the clans, and the youngest, but he is also willing to listen to God. That fact alone puts him at the head of the line! God looks for willing hearts. While Gideon doesn't understand the present "apparent" absence of God's power at work, he is at least talking to God.

Power of The Lord:

Judges 6:14-16 ~

[14] *The Lord turned to him and said, "Go in the strength you have and save Israel out of Midian's hand. Am I not sending you?"*
[15] *"Pardon me, my lord," Gideon replied, "but how can I save Israel? My clan is the weakest in Manasseh, and I am the least in my family."*
[16] *The Lord answered, "I will be with you, and you will strike down all the Midianites, leaving none alive."*

"Where is God's power when we need it?" Notice the wrong perspective here: Gideon didn't notice who it was who abandoned whom! God had not abandoned them; they had abandoned God! They had failed to talk to the right source before, and this will always fail to bring peace!

God could take their weakness, however, and reveal His power! Gideon was a nobody! Manasseh was a divided tribe. Gideon's clan was one of the weakest in Manasseh. Gideon himself was the youngest or least in the family. He was the lowest of the low!

Now God could reveal His power in their weakness! Notice that Gideon was still thinking like the present generation, that things were up to them.

Judges 6:15 ~

"But Lord," Gideon asked, "how can I save Israel?"

The underline in this verse is mine for emphasis, to illustrate a point. Gideon thought it would be up to him. God corrects this misunderstanding quickly, however.

Judges 6:16 ~

The LORD answered, "I will be with you, and you will strike down all the Midianites together."

It wouldn't be Gideon's power; it would be God's through him. God isn't concerned how weak or impossible our situation is. The worse it is, the clearer that it is His power and not ours that brings victory!

Promise of The Lord:

Judges 6:17-22 ~

[17]Gideon replied, "If now I have found favor in your

eyes, give me a sign that it is really you talking to me. [18]Please do not go away until I come back and bring my offering and set it before you."

And the Lord said, "I will wait until you return."

[19]Gideon went inside, prepared a young goat, and from an ephah of flour he made bread without yeast. Putting the meat in a basket and its broth in a pot, he brought them out and offered them to him under the oak.

[20]The angel of God said to him, "Take the meat and the unleavened bread, place them on this rock, and pour out the broth." And Gideon did so. [21]Then the angel of the Lord touched the meat and the unleavened bread with the tip of the staff that was in his hand. Fire flared from the rock, consuming the meat and the bread. And the angel of the Lord disappeared. [22]When Gideon realized that it was the angel of the Lord, he exclaimed, "Alas, Sovereign Lord! I have seen the angel of the Lord face to face!"

God gives His promise to be with him. God graciously promises to wait for Gideon to return. God is full of mercy. He promises to give him victory – Judges 6:19-22a – Gideon prepares a sacrifice and demonstrates the proper sense of giving here. Sacrifice is part of our relationship with God.

This is our promise that God is in control. Gideon

realizes, after all, that God is really in charge!

He marvels at having been in God's presence, this alone changes him ... and should us too.

PEACE!

Judges 6:23-24 ~

23But the Lord said to him, "Peace! Do not be afraid. You are not going to die." 24So Gideon built an altar to the Lord there and called it The Lord Is Peace. To this day it stands in Ophrah of the Abiezrites.

Now that Gideon has moved from problems, to priorities, to perspective, he can receive peace! Now God says to him, "Peace." Peace is the byproduct of a real relationship with God. When we are in right relationship with Him, we can sense His peace. God's power, instead of destroying our lives, gives us our life! Where fear once ruled, now peace rules the heart! But Gideon's peace came because God came into Gideon's life! The starting point of real peace is found in finding Christ as our Savior! "THE LORD IS PEACE!" (Jehovah-Shalom)

Peace Of God - "The Lord Is Peace" (Jehovah-Shalom)

Gideon builds an altar to God here and calls it: "The

Lord is Peace" (Jehovah-Shalom). Jesus in John 20:19-23 appears to the disciples as the resurrected Lord and twice says: "Peace be with you." That's because Jesus was with them, and He is our Peace!

No matter what shape the world is in, or what shape our personal lives are in, we can have peace now!

A friend visited an elderly woman badly crippled by arthritis. When asked, "Do you suffer much?" she responded, "Yes, but there is no nail here," and she pointed to her hand. "He had the nails, I have the peace." She pointed to her head. "There are no thorns here. He had the thorns, I have the peace." She touched her side. "There is no spear here. He had the spear, I have the peace." That is what the atonement of Jesus Christ means for us — He gave of himself so that we might have the peace.

Biblical peace is not the eradication of problems, but assurance of God's presence even in problems! The world can't offer this kind of peace! Theirs is based on solving problems; God's is based on saving people! This peace came to Gideon before victory on the battlefield! Our peace is found in God, not goods! The world tries to solve problems to bring peace; God saves people to bring peace! Which would you rather have, peaceful solutions, or peaceful souls? "THE LORD IS PEACE!" (Jehovah-Shalom).

— 4 —

JEHOVAH-JIREH

The Lord Will Provide &
the Lord Will See!

of the joys of being a father is the pleasure I get out of providing for my family. It is a joy to see my children healthy and happy — clothed, eating good food; these things I try and provide without their even asking.

It is also fun to provide something they ask for. To see them happy makes me happy, although sometimes I must keep something from them until their priorities are correct or until they are mature enough to handle what they are asking for, i.e., candy before supper, or a gun that cannot be given to a 5-year-old, etc.

The Scriptures teach us that God delights in being our provider; He is a good father who delights in His children and their happiness.

PROMISE TO PROVIDE

Salvation Provided:

Genesis 22:8, 14 ~

[8]*Abraham answered, "God himself will provide the lamb for the burnt offering, my son." And the two of them went on together.*
[14]*So Abraham called that place The Lord Will Provide. And to this day it is said, "On the mountain of the Lord it will be provided."*

This is the ultimate provision and the greatest gift! God's mercy saves us in this life. Then it saves us in the life to come. Without this provision, the material things have little meaning or joy! *"What does it profit a man if* he gains the world but loses his soul?" (Mark 8:36) God has not asked us to save ourselves; He will save us.

We have to climb up to Him to find freedom, for we cannot save ourselves. God provided the lamb. God desires to save us from sin, the world, and from ourselves!

Staples Promised:

Matthew 6:25-27 ~

[25] *"Therefore I tell you, do not worry about your life, what you will eat or drink; or about your body, what you will wear. Is not life more than food, and the body more than clothes?* [26]*Look at the birds of the air; they do not sow or reap or store away in barns, and yet your heavenly Father feeds them. Are you not much more valuable than they?* [27]*Can any one of you by worrying add a single hour to your life?"*

God is concerned about our basic needs: food and drink, clothing, shelter. God will provide these things. If the lesser things of creation are taken care of, will not God take care of the greatest of creation – man?!

If God attends the funeral of a sparrow, do you think he does not care for you and me? To not worry, however, doesn't mean that we should not work or do anything; God's Word tells us that the man who does not work shall not eat!

2 Thessalonians 3:10 ~

For even when we were with you, we gave you this rule: "If a man will not work, he shall not eat."

In fact, if we don't work or aren't willing to do our part, God may not provide these necessities! Work is part of the way God provides for us! Even the 4th commandment had two parts to it: *"Six days you shall labor and do all your work, but the seventh day is a Sabbath to the LORD your God."* (Ex. 20:9b-10a) God created man with two explicit natures: working and worshipping. Man the Worker – Man the Worshipper

PROVISION & PRIORITIES

Secure People:

Matthew 6:28-32 ~

[28] *"And why do you worry about clothes? See how the flowers of the field grow. They do not labor or spin.* [29] *Yet I tell you that not even Solomon in all his splendor was dressed like one of these.* [30] *If that is how God*

clothes the grass of the field, which is here today and tomorrow is thrown into the fire, will he not much more clothe you—you of little faith? *31*So do not worry, saying, 'What shall we eat?' or 'What shall we drink?' or 'What shall we wear?' *32*For the pagans run after all these things, and your heavenly Father knows that you need them."

Stop worrying! Do, however, plan for the future! Plants plan for the future by producing flowers that will yield seed or produce bulbs, but they do it without fretting over the future, which is the point! Birds plan for the future; they build nests and feed their young, but they do it without fretting! Worrying destroys – planning develops.

There is a difference between worry and concern. A worried person sees the problem; the concerned person solves the problem. Worry consumes good energy and accomplishes nothing!

Matthew 6:27 ~

"Who of you by worrying can add a single hour to his life?"

Planning, however, is productive and utilizes energy. God is not opposed to good planning, just against useless fretting over the future! The world frets.

Matthew 6:32 ~

"For the pagans run after all these things, and your heavenly Father knows that you need them."

Second Place!

Matthew 6:33 ~

"But seek first his kingdom and his righteousness, and all these things will be given to you as well."

God's provisions will be granted if our priorities are correct! Remember, the candy doesn't come before supper! Many times, our frustrations over our needs may be the result of not having put God first place in our lives! God comes first! This was the idea in the Old Testament behind God getting the first fruits! When God is first, then God puts us first as well! All these other things that we need are provided. God gives to givers! (He may even take joy in giving beyond our needs when He sees that nothing in our heart takes His being first place!)

Augustine said, "God is more anxious to bestow his blessings on us than we are to receive them."

PROVIDING BY PETITION

Some Persistence:

Luke 18:1-5 ~

[1]Then Jesus told his disciples a parable to show them that they should always pray and not give up. [2]He said: "In a certain town there was a judge who neither feared God nor cared what people thought. [3]And there was a widow in that town who kept coming to him with the plea, 'Grant me justice against my adversary.'

[4]"For some time he refused. But finally, he said to himself, 'Even though I don't fear God or care what people think, [5]yet because this widow keeps bothering me, I will see that she gets justice, so that she won't eventually come and attack me!'"

Jewish concept was that praying more than three times a day made God weary ... thus you shouldn't ask more than three times a day. They based this idea on Daniel having prayed three times a day. Jesus here was only using their concept as a case in point on persistence, not supporting their misguided concept. He was trying to say to them that their concept may cause them to miss some of God's blessing, that persistence may bring an answer. God sometimes wants us to persist in prayer!

Never give up until you get an answer from God! Praying develops spiritual muscles! God may have reasons for having us persist in prayer before answering. Maybe to develop a burden. Maybe to test our sincerity. Maybe to help us appreciate the answer more. Perhaps it makes us serious about the need. Maybe the time is not right for the answer. Maybe to teach us responsibility and practice balanced living, too!

Savior's Plans:

Luke 18:6, 7 ~

[6]*And the Lord said, "Listen to what the unjust judge says. [7]And will not God bring about justice for his chosen ones, who cry out to him day and night? Will he keep putting them off?"*

Chosen ones, persistence demonstrates our concern. God answers in His time reference, not ours. When we worry, we believe more in our problems than in God's promises. His perspective is eternal. Ours too often is temporal.

Strength & Patience:

Luke 18:8 ~

"I tell you, he will see that they get justice, and quickly. However, when the Son of Man comes, will he find faith on the earth?"

Persistence makes us strong. It develops our faith! It even gives us an appreciation for His answers and who He is.

Be persistent, and God will bless you with patience! And when patience has had its work, it makes us mature, lacking nothing. We need not worry about our needs in this life if we have put God first; He is a faithful Father who provides for His children! He is still Jehovah-Jireh!

— 5 —

JEHOVAH-SHADDAI

The All Sufficient & All Powerful One

claims for being powerful are many today:

~ Excedrin claims that it has extra strength! (So do others!)

~ Comet cleanser is the "powerful one!"

~ Cheer has more whitening power than all other

brands.

~ America is the most powerful nation in the world.

~ Superman is more powerful than a locomotive.

~ Hefty is stronger than the 1- or 2-ply bags.

~ Polident is more powerful than coffee stains or blueberries.

~ Nations are scrambling to become "nuclear powers" so they can be thought of as "all powerful" and feared.

YET: No matter who or what claims to be "all powerful," the best they can claim is to be only "more powerful!" They still all fall short of God's "all power-ful" status!

The Scripture tells us that God and God alone is the "almighty one," the "all powerful" over all things, and in Him we are victorious and strong!

POWER OVER PROBLEMS

Exodus 6:2-3 ~

²God also said to Moses, "I am the Lord. ³I appeared to Abraham, to Isaac and to Jacob as God Almighty, but by my name the Lord I did not make myself fully known to them."

James 1:13-15 ~

13When tempted, no one should say, "God is tempting me." For God cannot be tempted by evil, nor does he tempt anyone; 14but each person is tempted when they are dragged away by their own evil desire and enticed. 15Then, after desire has conceived, it gives birth to sin; and sin, when it is full-grown, gives birth to death.

Problem of Sin:

Romans 3:23 says that *"all have sinned."* This is man's greatest problem! The problem of food or energy is only temporary. We face the quandary of eternal vs. temporal problems. Food, energy, etc. affect only the now; sin affects eternity as well as the now! If sin were conquered we could also conquer the other problems that are temporal! When the sin issue is dealt with in our hearts through God's power, many of the things that once held us in bondage can finally change because God's power is at work in us and through us.

Rochester, New York, was dramatically transformed by Charles Finney's work there in 1830-31 in what has been called the greatest year of spiritual awakening in American history. Shops were closed so people could attend his meetings, and as a result of the changed hearts, the town taverns went out of business. Finney soon won international fame. The world's greatest problem is not the poverty of goods, but the poverty of God! John 3:16 tells us that the problem of sin has been overpowered by God Almighty. God made a plan for man's sin to be conquered. Jesus Himself paid the price; man could not do so. For God's people, it does not have to be a problem any longer!

Problem of Satan:

John 3:16 ~

For God so loved the world that he gave his one and only Son, that whoever believes in him shall not perish but have eternal life.

Sometimes it seems that Satan is winning. This world has been ruled by him, and he has been a problem, you know! But: Jesus has power over him! Satan is no problem to God! He is a nuisance, not a winner! Christ has taken from him the keys of death and hell. Christ has overpowered Satan! Satan is not a problem for the Saint, only the sinner! Even if the Christian appears not to change the world overnight, he can change the world one day at a time by simply plodding forward in God's power.

When William Carey began thinking of going to

India as a pioneer missionary, his father pointed out to him that he possessed no academic qualifications that would fit him for such a task. But Carey answered, "I can plod." How true it is that God accomplishes mighty things for His kingdom through those who are willing to persevere, who are willing to plod faithfully through one difficulty after another in the power of the Spirit. God's power works in us one day at a time. Satan is a temporary problem, a problem that will ultimately be terminated!

Problem of Self:

James 1:13-15 ~

13When tempted, no one should say, "God is tempting me." For God cannot be tempted by evil, nor does he tempt anyone; 14but each person is tempted when they are dragged away by their own evil desire and enticed. 15Then, after desire has conceived, it gives birth to sin; and sin, when it is full-grown, gives birth to death.

Most of our trouble with sin does not come from Satan, but self! This world has a "The devil made me do it" mentality. We often try and blame others or Satan for our sins, when it really boils down to self most of the time! We are our own worst enemy! We are drawn away by our own lusts. Fallen nature is at work in us! Sinful desires lead to sin if we fulfill them! We don't sin because we have to but because we want to! Sometimes we don't utilize the resources we have in God's power to overcome, and thus fail to live in victory.

Stephen Blankenship wrote of a New Year's Day Tournament of Roses parade in which a beautiful float suddenly sputtered and quit. It was out of gas. The whole parade was held up until someone could get a can of gas. The amusing thing was that this float represented the Standard Oil Company. With its vast oil resources, its truck was out of gas. Often, Christians neglect their spiritual maintenance, and though they are *"clothed with power"* (Luke 24:49), they run out of gas in the Lord.

God's power in us gives us power over our fallen nature. We don't have to yield to sin with God's Spirit helping us to become an overcomer! God's power is greater than our sins. We can be victorious and say "no" to sin ... God's power lives in us ... the Almighty Himself is our Lord — no longer our self!

POWER OVER PEOPLE

People of Schemes:

Daniel 6:1-24 ~

¹It pleased Darius to appoint 120 satraps to rule

throughout the kingdom, [2]with three administrators over them, one of whom was Daniel. The satraps were made accountable to them so that the king might not suffer loss. [3]Now Daniel so distinguished himself among the administrators and the satraps by his exceptional qualities that the king planned to set him over the whole kingdom. [4]At this, the administrators and the satraps tried to find grounds for charges against Daniel in his conduct of government affairs, but they were unable to do so. They could find no corruption in him, because he was trustworthy and neither corrupt nor negligent. [5]Finally these men said, "We will never find any basis for charges against this man Daniel unless it has something to do with the law of his God."

[6]So these administrators and satraps went as a group to the king and said: "May King Darius live forever! [7]The royal administrators, prefects, satraps, advisers and governors have all agreed that the king should issue an edict and enforce the decree that anyone who prays to any god or human being during the next thirty days, except to you, Your Majesty, shall be thrown into the lions' den. [8]Now, Your Majesty, issue the decree and put it in writing so that it cannot be altered—in accordance with the law of the Medes and Persians, which cannot be repealed." [9]So King Darius put the decree in writing.

[10]Now when Daniel learned that the decree had been published, he went home to his upstairs room where the

windows opened toward Jerusalem. Three times a day he got down on his knees and prayed, giving thanks to his God, just as he had done before. [11] Then these men went as a group and found Daniel praying and asking God for help. [12] So they went to the king and spoke to him about his royal decree: "Did you not publish a decree that during the next thirty days anyone who prays to any god or human being except to you, Your Majesty, would be thrown into the lions' den?"

The king answered, "The decree stands—in accordance with the law of the Medes and Persians, which cannot be repealed."

[13] Then they said to the king, "Daniel, who is one of the exiles from Judah, pays no attention to you, Your Majesty, or to the decree you put in writing. He still prays three times a day." [14] When the king heard this, he was greatly distressed; he was determined to rescue Daniel and made every effort until sundown to save him.

[15] Then the men went as a group to King Darius and said to him, "Remember, Your Majesty, that according to the law of the Medes and Persians no decree or edict that the king issues can be changed."

[16] So the king gave the order, and they brought Daniel and threw him into the lions' den. The king said to Daniel, "May your God, whom you serve continually, rescue you!"

[17] A stone was brought and placed over the mouth of

the den, and the king sealed it with his own signet ring and with the rings of his nobles, so that Daniel's situation might not be changed. *18* Then the king returned to his palace and spent the night without eating and without any entertainment being brought to him. And he could not sleep.

19 At the first light of dawn, the king got up and hurried to the lions' den. *20* When he came near the den, he called to Daniel in an anguished voice, "Daniel, servant of the living God, has your God, whom you serve continually, been able to rescue you from the lions?"

21 Daniel answered, "May the king live forever! *22* My God sent his angel, and he shut the mouths of the lions. They have not hurt me, because I was found innocent in his sight. Nor have I ever done any wrong before you, Your Majesty."

23 The king was overjoyed and gave orders to lift Daniel out of the den. And when Daniel was lifted from the den, no wound was found on him, because he had trusted in his God.

24 At the king's command, the men who had falsely accused Daniel were brought in and thrown into the lions' den, along with their wives and children. And before they reached the floor of the den, the lions overpowered them and crushed all their bones.

Those that would try and destroy us may appear to

be successful at times. But in the end, they will be conquered by God's power and plan. Daniel appeared to have lost by those who schemed against him. We need not fear man, even evil men! God will keep us in His power. Daniel was delivered. Daniel was weak and old, but God was still almighty. Daniel here may have been between 70 and his mid-90s! – he was most likely in his early 90s! When you get involved in the story of God's power, it affects you! Daniel's schemers were thrown to the lions, their own evil came back to them ... usually true of those who try and hurt others! (Dan. 6:24)

People of Sin:

Daniel 6:25-28 ~

[25] *Then King Darius wrote to all the nations and peoples of every language in all the earth: "May you prosper greatly!* [26] *I issue a decree that in every part of my kingdom people must fear and reverence the God of Daniel. For he is the living God and he endures forever; his kingdom will not be destroyed, his dominion will never end.* [27] *He rescues and he saves; he performs signs and wonders in the heavens and on the earth. He has rescued Daniel from the power of the lions."*

[28] *So Daniel prospered during the reign of Darius and the reign of Cyrus the Persian.*

Man does not ultimately rule the world; God does! Even King Darius finally recognized this and wrote a decree that there was no other God like Daniel's God, that only He was all powerful. If an earthly king can write the following: *"For he is the living God and he endures forever; his kingdom will not be destroyed, his dominion will never end. He rescues and he saves; he performs signs and wonders in the heavens and on the earth. He has rescued Daniel from the power of the lions."* – How much more should we recognize His almighty power? Sinners may feel powerful with bombs and large armies, but God's power is almighty!

While there is a lot of terror going on in the world today, we must remember that God is still very much in control. Sinful man will not determine the future ... God will do this.

We must not lose heart about tomorrow; God has everything in control, even the affairs of sinful man.

POWER OVER

Plans of Satan:

Exodus 13:17-14:31 ~

[17] *When Pharaoh let the people go, God did not lead*

them on the road through the Philistine country, though that was shorter. For God said, "If they face war, they might change their minds and return to Egypt." ¹⁸So God led the people around by the desert road toward the Red Sea. The Israelites went up out of Egypt ready for battle.

¹⁹Moses took the bones of Joseph with him because Joseph had made the Israelites swear an oath. He had said, "God will surely come to your aid, and then you must carry my bones up with you from this place."

²⁰After leaving Sukkoth they camped at Etham on the edge of the desert. ²¹By day the Lord went ahead of them in a pillar of cloud to guide them on their way and by night in a pillar of fire to give them light, so that they could travel by day or night. ²²Neither the pillar of cloud by day nor the pillar of fire by night left its place in front of the people.

¹Then the Lord said to Moses, ²"Tell the Israelites to turn back and encamp near Pi Hahiroth, between Migdol and the sea. They are to encamp by the sea, directly opposite Baal Zephon. ³Pharaoh will think, 'The Israelites are wandering around the land in confusion, hemmed in by the desert.' ⁴And I will harden Pharaoh's heart, and he will pursue them. But I will gain glory for myself through Pharaoh and all his army, and the Egyptians will know that I am the Lord." So the Israelites did this.

⁵When the king of Egypt was told that the people had fled, Pharaoh and his officials changed their minds about them and said, "What have we done? We have let the Israelites go and have lost their services!" ⁶So he had his chariot made ready and took his army with him. ⁷He took six hundred of the best chariots, along with all the other chariots of Egypt, with officers over all of them. ⁸The Lord hardened the heart of Pharaoh king of Egypt, so that he pursued the Israelites, who were marching out boldly. ⁹The Egyptians—all Pharaoh's horses and chariots, horsemen and troops—pursued the Israelites and overtook them as they camped by the sea near Pi Hahiroth, opposite Baal Zephon.

¹⁰As Pharaoh approached, the Israelites looked up, and there were the Egyptians, marching after them. They were terrified and cried out to the Lord. ¹¹They said to Moses, "Was it because there were no graves in Egypt that you brought us to the desert to die? What have you done to us by bringing us out of Egypt? ¹²Didn't we say to you in Egypt, 'Leave us alone; let us serve the Egyptians'? It would have been better for us to serve the Egyptians than to die in the desert!"

¹³Moses answered the people, "Do not be afraid. Stand firm and you will see the deliverance the Lord will bring you today. The Egyptians you see today you will never see again. ¹⁴The Lord will fight for you; you need only to be still."

¹⁵ Then the Lord said to Moses, "Why are you crying out to me? Tell the Israelites to move on. ¹⁶ Raise your staff and stretch out your hand over the sea to divide the water so that the Israelites can go through the sea on dry ground. ¹⁷ I will harden the hearts of the Egyptians so that they will go in after them. And I will gain glory through Pharaoh and all his army, through his chariots and his horsemen. ¹⁸ The Egyptians will know that I am the Lord when I gain glory through Pharaoh, his chariots and his horsemen."

¹⁹ Then the angel of God, who had been traveling in front of Israel's army, withdrew and went behind them. The pillar of cloud also moved from in front and stood behind them, ²⁰ coming between the armies of Egypt and Israel. Throughout the night the cloud brought darkness to the one side and light to the other side; so neither went near the other all night long.

²¹ Then Moses stretched out his hand over the sea, and all that night the Lord drove the sea back with a strong east wind and turned it into dry land. The waters were divided, ²² and the Israelites went through the sea on dry ground, with a wall of water on their right and on their left.

²³ The Egyptians pursued them, and all Pharaoh's horses and chariots and horsemen followed them into the sea. ²⁴ During the last watch of the night the Lord looked down from the pillar of fire and cloud at the

Egyptian army and threw it into confusion. ^{25}He jammed the wheels of their chariots so that they had difficulty driving. And the Egyptians said, "Let's get away from the Israelites! The Lord is fighting for them against Egypt."

^{26}Then the Lord said to Moses, "Stretch out your hand over the sea so that the waters may flow back over the Egyptians and their chariots and horsemen." ^{27}Moses stretched out his hand over the sea, and at daybreak the sea went back to its place. The Egyptians were fleeing toward it, and the Lord swept them into the sea. ^{28}The water flowed back and covered the chariots and horsemen—the entire army of Pharaoh that had followed the Israelites into the sea. Not one of them survived.

^{29}But the Israelites went through the sea on dry ground, with a wall of water on their right and on their left. ^{30}That day the Lord saved Israel from the hands of the Egyptians, and Israel saw the Egyptians lying dead on the shore. ^{31}And when the Israelites saw the mighty hand of the Lord displayed against the Egyptians, the people feared the Lord and put their trust in him and in Moses his servant.

Pharaoh had it all figured out: He decided what he was going to do ... and so had God!!!

Oswald Chambers wrote, the remarkable thing about fearing God is that when you fear God, you fear nothing else, whereas if you do not fear God, you fear everything else. Satan's plans always end in destruction. God's always end in construction. God puts down one ruler and lifts up another. Satan's plans for this world will not be successful! Pharaoh assumed he was more powerful than God. This was a bad assumption, and in the end cost him a great deal ... including the life of his first-born son.

Satan always tries to make us believe we are our own master, that we have control over ourselves. In the end, this will prove a disaster, however. Satan's original temptation for Adam and Eve was to tempt them to be "like" God, so that they could be His equal. It failed then, and it will fail now. Satan's plans are always frustrated by God's power! Jesus dying on the cross at first seemed to be Satan's victory! But Jesus' cry from the cross was a hint that Satan was losing already. Jesus cried, "It is finished" – and this was not a cry of defeat. It was an accounting term which meant, "Paid in full." Jesus was already hinting that He had paid it all, and that sin was over as the master of the human race. Now there would be freedom for humans who chose to accept Christ. Then Christ arose ... defeating not only Satan, but sin!

Plans of Self:

James 4:13-17 ~

[13]Now listen, you who say, "Today or tomorrow we will go to this or that city, spend a year there, carry on business and make money." [14]Why, you do not even know what will happen tomorrow. What is your life? You are a mist that appears for a little while and then vanishes. [15]Instead, you ought to say, "If it is the Lord's will, we will live and do this or that." [16]As it is, you boast in your arrogant schemes. All such boasting is evil. [17]If anyone, then, knows the good they ought to do and doesn't do it, it is sin for them.

God is greater than our plans. Ultimately, our plans are only as good as God's will allows. His power is greater than our program! In this sense we can only expect our plans to work if we realize that they are subject to God's approval, not ours! God's power keeps us from some of our plans, THANK GOD! His power protects us and keeps us. He alone is powerful enough to override our plans! It is not wrong to plan for tomorrow, but we must realize God is in control! We are subject to Him, not He to us!

God alone is Almighty! He is greater than our problems, than any person, and any plan of man's or of Satan's! He is the Lord God Almighty! "JEHOVAH-SHADDAI!"

— 6 —

JEHOVAH-TSIDKENU

The Lord our Righteousness!

Have you ever met someone who likes to remind you or tell you how spiritual they are? They can do this in many different ways:

1. By pointing out how unspiritual you are, or at least hinting at it.

2. By telling you how much they give to the Lord, or how many gifts of the Spirit they possess, etc.

3. By telling you of how close they are with some giants of the faith, Billy Graham, David Wilkerson, etc.

4. By telling you how many different important positions they have held in God's work or the church.

We cannot win success by attaching ourselves to the wrong source!

The Bible teaches us that Jesus Christ is our Righteousness, not our works, nor the gifts we possess, nor our friendship with giants of faith. It is our relationship to Jesus, the Lord our Righteousness!

RIGHTEOUS RULER

Right Living:

Jeremiah 23:5-6 ~

[5]*"The days are coming," declares the Lord, "when I will raise up for David a righteous Branch, a King who will reign wisely and do what is just and right in the land. [6]In his days Judah will be saved and Israel will live in safety. This is the name by which he will be called: The Lord Our Righteous Savior."*

Since no man since Adam had lived sinless, how

could man become "righteous" before God? It was going to require something unique. No regular stuff would work. Man needed a ruler who would live right. No one had completely done this before, but God promised that someone would, a ruler who would live righteously. Before God. Before man. He would be wise.

In His day there would be salvation. He would be the "Lord Our Righteousness." He would bring us into right relationship to God. This is the idea of righteousness: a right standing before God. This destroys the idea that righteousness can be achieved by our own deeds or works; it will be accomplished through a relationship through this ruler.

Restored Life:

Jeremiah 23:7-8 ~

[7] *"So then, the days are coming," declares the Lord, "when people will no longer say, 'As surely as the Lord lives, who brought the Israelites up out of Egypt,'* [8] *but they will say, 'As surely as the Lord lives, who brought the descendants of Israel up out of the land of the north and out of all the countries where he had banished them.' Then they will live in their own land."*

As great as the deliverance of Israel from Egypt was,

this Ruler's deliverance would be even greater! The former gave Israel a new land, the latter a new life! Moses led them toward new property, Jesus would give them a new position. The former glory will be nothing compared to the latter. The new righteousness from the new ruler would greatly outdo the old righteousness.

It won't be our efforts or wealth or position that get us into this new life; it will be the "NEW RULER" Himself that will do this.

It's been said that a person may go to heaven without health, without riches, without honors, without learning, without friends; but he can never go there without Christ. Restored life is available for all who accept this righteous ruler ... JESUS CHRIST!

RIGHTEOUSNESS RECEIVED

Received the Lord:

Colossians 2:6-7 ~

[6]*So then, just as you received Christ Jesus as Lord, continue to live your lives in him, [7]rooted and built up in him, strengthened in the faith as you were taught, and overflowing with thankfulness.*

Jesus is not only the starting point of righteousness,

but the continual flow of it! We cannot be righteous without Christ! Only His robes of righteousness are large enough to cover our filthy rags.

In the days of horse and buggies, a father went to the schoolhouse to pick up his three children ages 9, 11, and 17. As soon as he had them in the buggy — just before he stepped in — probably out of fear of the storm, the horses bolted and took off in the blizzard. Hours and miles later, when he found his children, the 17-year-old girl stood over the dead and frozen bodies of her brother and sister, 9 and 11. Sobbing uncontrollably, she collapsed into his arms. When she had regained her composure, she explained to her father that she tried to take her big, heavy coat and wrap it around them all. But she said, "The coat wasn't big enough." The blood that Christ shed on the cross is big enough to cover all of your sins and mine — all your lusting, all your lying, all your cheating, all your hatred, all your own faults.

We — *I* — must always depend on Christ to keep in right standing before God!! He is to be Lord of all my life, or He is not Lord at all in my life! He is my constant source of righteousness! Not my good works, efforts, positions, etc. This is what produces thankfulness. He has done it! (Otherwise, I could thank myself!) It is Christ's garment of righteousness that we wear, not our own.

Don't disgrace this beautiful garment of righteousness. Joseph wore the "coat of many colors" and his brethren became mad and jealous ... it was a coat his father had given him and later was instrumental in God's plan for his life. That coat changed Joseph's life, and so should the coat of Christ's righteousness change ours.

Rejecting Lies:

Colossians 2:8 ~

See to it that no one takes you captive through hollow and deceptive philosophy, which depends on human tradition and the elemental spiritual forces of this world rather than on Christ.

The world judges goodness by what it sets up as the standards of goodness. Its philosophies change from generation to generation. Its ideas of morality change constantly concerning sexuality and murder. Convenience rules. Its traditions are empty of satisfaction. As God's people, righteousness cannot and must not be determined by this world or its standards, but by Christ and His Word!

Billy Graham once said that we've lost sight of the fact that some things are always right and some things are always wrong. We've lost our reference point. We don't have any moral philosophy to undergird our way of life in this country, and our way of life is in serious jeopardy unless something happens. And that something must be a spiritual revival.

We are to reject this world's thinking and standards that don't line up with Christ's! (Even when this world makes its standards sound so reasonable!) They may even be logically convincing ... but they are still lies if they contradict the Word of God! Ever met a liar that is convincing?

Righteous Life:

Mark Twain said, "Heaven goes by favor. If it went by merit, you would stay out, and your dog would go in."

In Christ, we have it all. Colossians 2:10 tells us that *"in Christ you have been brought to fullness."* He is the head over every power and authority. All the righteousness we need we have in Christ. Christ Jesus is our righteousness. In Him we are accepted and clean! In Christ, the work of righteousness is complete!

Colossians 2:11-15 ~

[11]In him you were also circumcised with a circumcision not performed by human hands. Your whole self ruled by the flesh was put off when you were

circumcised by Christ, [12]having been buried with him in baptism, in which you were also raised with him through your faith in the working of God, who raised him from the dead.

[13]When you were dead in your sins and in the uncircumcision of your flesh, God made you alive with Christ. He forgave us all our sins, [14]having canceled the charge of our legal indebtedness, which stood against us and condemned us; he has taken it away, nailing it to the cross. [15]And having disarmed the powers and authorities, he made a public spectacle of them, triumphing over them by the cross.

It's been said that the difference between religion and salvation is that religion is man trying to do something for God — salvation is God doing something for man. Praise God we have a righteous life! We can live free from condemnation! Now we overflow with thank-fulness.

RIGHTEOUSNESS RULING

Regulations are Lifeless:

Religious motions don't give us righteousness!

Colossians 2:16 ~

Therefore do not let anyone judge you by what you eat or drink, or with regard to a religious festival, a New Moon celebration or a Sabbath day.

The repeated promises in the Qur'an of the forgiveness of a compassionate and merciful Allah are all made to the meritorious, whose merits have been weighed in Allah's scales, whereas the Gospel is good news of mercy to the undeserving. The symbol of the religion of Jesus is the cross, not the scales. Unlike other religions that require you to "earn" your righteousness, we receive ours in Christ as a gift! Jesus paid the price for our righteousness. The Old Testament laws and practices were all shadows of truth to be found in Christ and in his sacrifice on the cross.

Colossians 2:17 ~

These are a shadow of the things that were to come; the reality, however, is found in Christ.

~ The temple
~ The sacrifices
~ The festivals

Don't let others fool you by making you believe they are more righteous than you.

Colossians 2:18 ~

Do not let anyone who delights in false humility and the worship of angels disqualify you. Such a person also goes into great detail about what they have seen; they are puffed up with idle notions by their unspiritual mind.

In Christ we are all righteous together! We are either in Christ or not, righteous or not, Saint or sinner! False humility is really covered-up pride! The one who brags on his righteousness has lost touch with God!

Colossians 2:19 ~

They have lost connection with the head, from whom the whole body, supported and held together by its ligaments and sinews, grows as God causes it to grow.

Quit trying to be righteous by what you do, rather do because you are righteous in Christ!

Colossians 2:20-23 ~

[20]Since you died with Christ to the elemental spiritual forces of this world, why, as though you still belonged to the world, do you submit to its rules: [21]"Do

not handle! Do not taste! Do not touch!"? ²²These rules, which have to do with things that are all destined to perish with use, are based on merely human commands and teachings. ²³Such regulations indeed have an appearance of wisdom, with their self-imposed worship, their false humility and their harsh treatment of the body, but they lack any value in restraining sensual indulgence.

Regulations won't control sinful appetites. Righteousness will control sinful appetites.

Wayne Jacobsen once said, "Spiritual authority flows not from titles and positions but from a life that is genuine." This is the secret to overcoming a sinful habit; quit trying to do it by law and regulations; rather, let Christ's righteousness be your strength!

Resurrection Living:

Colossians 3:1-4 ~

¹Since, then, you have been raised with Christ, set your hearts on things above, where Christ is, seated at the right hand of God. ²Set your minds on things above, not on earthly things. ³For you died, and your life is now hidden with Christ in God. ⁴When Christ, who is your life, appears, then you also will appear with him in glory.

Set your hearts on things above! Don't live in such a way that you have to be ruled by the things of this life. Take away fretting over this life. Christ is our life ... resurrection life begins now — not just in the future.

Somebody asked a Christian, "Are you saved?" "In what tense?" was the strange retort of the Christian. "What do you mean?" "Well," said the Christian, "salvation is in three tenses: it is in the past: *'Not by works of righteousness which we have done, but according to his mercy he saved us, by the washing of regeneration, and renewing of the Holy Ghost'* (Titus 3:5). Here is salvation in the present: *'Moreover, brethren, I declare unto you the gospel which I preached unto you, which also ye have received, and ... by which also ye are saved.'* The Greek word 'sozesthe' is inadequately translated in the King James Version. It should be *'ye are being saved'* (I Cor. 15:2). Not only were we saved in the past, but we need salvation continuously. Finally, there is salvation in the future: *'Much more then, being now justified by his blood, we shall be saved from wrath through him'* (Rom. 5:9)."

Is your salvation in all three tenses?

We are alive in Christ, not dead in sins, with resurrection life flowing through us now!

The Bible teaches us that Christ is our righteousness, not our works, nor the gifts we possess, nor our friendships with giants of faith, nor our positions in the church. It is our relationship to Jesus ... THE "LORD OUR RIGHTEOUSNESS!" (Jehovah-Tsidkenu).

JEHOVAH-SHAMMAH

The Lord Is There!

Have

you ever gone through a great difficulty and felt like you were alone, that even God didn't care or hear you, that He had even abandoned you? Have you cried out to God, feeling like He wasn't interested and there never seems to be an answer to your cry, your struggle? You pray, you beg God ... but nothing!?

If you have ever felt this way, you are in good company ... men like David experienced this ... Moses knew the feeling, Job knew it, Peter and the other disciples went through this after Jesus' crucifixion. Paul said everyone had abandoned him at one point (2 Tim. 4:16), Elijah felt that he was alone ... he hid because he was afraid that he too would die just like he thought all the other prophets had (Rom. 11:2-5). Even Jesus felt the emotion of abandonment, first by His disciples, and then by God the Father when He was alone on the cross; He cried, "My God, My God, why hast thou forsaken me?" ... you see you are in good company when you experience this pain, yes, the pain of feeling alone ... but do not forget this one fact: GOD IS THERE ... no matter how you feel!

It's been said that we should never fear shadows. That just means a light's shining somewhere nearby. The Bible teaches us that God's presence is more than just a feeling, it is a reality of fact. THE "LORD IS THERE" NO MATTER WHAT WE THINK OR SENSE OR FEEL!

IN TIMES OF TEARS

Feelings of Being Forsaken:

Psalm 22:1 ~

My God, my God, why have you forsaken me? Why are you so far from saving me, so far from the words of my groaning?

David felt alone! He wondered if God really cared. His faith was low when his feelings were high! He could not understand how or why God allowed bad stuff to happen to him! Why doesn't God hear him and be there? This is a rather common experience among believers at some point in their walk with God. Even Jesus experienced this on the cross ... He quoted from this verse when hanging on the cross.

Frustration and Fear:

Psalm 22:2 ~

O my God, I cry out by day, but you do not answer, by night, and am not silent.

Left at this stage, despair and bitterness will set in and continue to develop. We might lose a proper perspective of God at this point; we might forget that although we don't feel His presence, He is still there. This is the natural result of letting one's feelings take over! Fear drives us away from God ... ("God has not given us the spirit of fear ..." 2 Tim. 1:7); ("Perfect love casts out all fear" ... I John 4:18).

Max Lucado said, "Fear doesn't want you to make the journey to the mountain. If he can rattle you enough, fear will persuade you to take your eyes off the peaks and settle for a dull existence in the flatlands."

Frustration left to develop leads to fear! And fear developed leaves us feeling alone and abandoned by God. Most of us do the dumb stuff at this stage; it is here that we often make the wrong choices.

Focusing on Facts:

Psalm 22:3-5 ~

³Yet you are enthroned as the Holy One; you are the one Israel praises. ⁴In you our ancestors put their trust; they trusted and you delivered them. ⁵To you they cried out and were saved; in you they trusted and were not put to shame.

God is on the throne — always! People in the past trusted in God and were saved! Israel cried out for 430 years in Egypt for deliverance. God did deliver them. God didn't disappoint them; He was there, even in their captivity! God is the same yesterday, today and forever!

IN TIMES OF TROUBLE

Faith in the Father:

In Psalm 22:6-11, David asks where this great God is now that he needs him. Despised by others and forsaken, made fun of ... David hangs onto his faith in God in this time of trouble.

Psalm 22:9-10 ~

⁹Yet you brought me out of the womb; you made me trust in you, even at my mother's breast. ¹⁰From birth I was cast on you; from my mother's womb you have been my God.

God was there before. He had never forsaken him before. When no one else can help, God will be there!

Psalm 22:11 ~

Do not be far from me, for trouble is near and there is no one to help.

Fretful & Fainthearted:

Nothing seems to be going right!

Psalm 22:12-14 ~

[12]Many bulls surround me; strong bulls of Bashan encircle me. [13]Roaring lions that tear their prey open their mouths wide against me. [14]I am poured out like water, and all my bones are out of joint. My heart has turned to wax; it has melted within me.

Everything is falling apart. Nobody understands. No one cares. Everyone has abandoned David or they are against him. He has no more strength left!

Psalm 22:15 ~

My strength is dried up like a potsherd, and my tongue sticks to the roof of my mouth; you lay me in the dust of death.

David was at his wit's end, and he asked God to be near.

Psalm 22:19-21 ~

[19]But you, Lord, do not be far from me. You are my strength; come quickly to help me. [20]Deliver me from the

sword, my precious life from the power of the dogs. [21]Rescue me from the mouth of the lions; save me from the horns of the wild oxen.

He is near and will stay near! God never leaves us nor forsakes us; God is there in the time of trouble! Give Him the time to work it out, in His time, not yours! Keep trusting in Him; don't fret unless you plan to faint!

IN TIMES OF TESTING

Footsteps of Faith:

Declare His name anyway!

Psalm 22:22 ~

I will declare your name to my brothers; in the congregation I will praise you.

Keep going to church and being with God's people! Keep praising God in spite of your feelings.

Psalm 22:23 ~

You who fear the LORD, praise him! All you descendants of Jacob, honor him! Revere him, all you descendants of Israel!

Faith gives a new focus — He has not left us; HE IS THERE!

Psalm 22:24b ~

... he has not hidden his face from him but has listened to his cry for help.

Following Faithfulness:

Psalm 22:25b ~

... before those who fear you will I fulfill my vows.

Fulfilling vows to God in front of all others; doing for God what we said we would do ... despite the circumstances and trials, is vital! Don't be quitters! This is also true of the vows we make to God's people. Follow through and be faithful!

In marriage we don't quit when the going gets tough; we promised to be faithful in sickness and health, riches or poor, etc. We stay faithful! This is true with God as well!

Our faithfulness despite how we feel will result in God's blessing on others and their praise in God.

Psalm 22:26 ~

The poor will eat and be satisfied; those who seek the Lord will praise him—may your hearts live forever!

Instead of following how we feel, we act in faith, trusting in God instead of how we feel at the time. We do this in our relationships with those we love all the time ... or we wouldn't have any relationships left on earth! If we acted out our feelings every time we felt like it, we would have no friends left. Instead, we discipline our actions in moments when our feelings are flowing strongly. We realize that our actions must be guided by more than our feelings. This is how we build a healthy marriage and friendships, and it is how we walk with God also.

Faith for the Future:

Psalm 22:27-31 ~

[27]*All the ends of the earth will remember and turn to the Lord, and all the families of the nations will bow down before him,* [28]*for dominion belongs to the Lord and he rules over the nations.* [29]*All the rich of the earth will feast and worship; all who go down to the dust will*

kneel before him—those who cannot keep themselves alive. [30]Posterity will serve him; future generations will be told about the Lord. [31]They will proclaim his righteousness, declaring to a people yet unborn: He has done it!

God was there in the past. God is here in the present. God will be there in the future!

The world will one day recognize His presence! Many will see the "LORD IS THERE!" Those yet to come will know God is there for His people!

No matter how alone we feel, or how frustrated we become with trials, how fearful or tearful, the fact remains — GOD IS THERE! He will never leave us nor forsake us! Let this fact rule your life, not your feelings!

— 8 —

JEHOVAH-ELYON

The Lord God Most High!

things we hold dearest, we hold highest in our hearts and minds:

~ America: The greatest country in our hearts has caused some to give their greatest sacrifice — their lives!

~ Family: Parents have died to save their children,

those they hold highest in their hearts.

~ Men have given up kingdoms for the women they loved and held highest in their hearts.

~ You can tell what a man or woman holds highest in their hearts by the devotion and sacrifices they give to whatever that is!

How we decide our budgets and our priorities says a lot about us ... and these things are more than just secular pursuits. It only takes a small amount of silver to obscure our view of others and their needs and what God wants us to see. We must be careful to remember that material things are simply temporal in nature, not eternal. The lure for the "stuff" of this world can quickly obscure our view of spiritual realities no matter how well intended we are.

One day a wealthy old miser visited a rabbi who took him by the hand and led him to a window. "Look out there," he said, pointing to the street. "What do you see?" "I see men and women and little children," answered the rich man. Again the rabbi took him by the hand and led him to the mirror and said, "What do you see now?" "Now I see myself," the rich man replied. Then the rabbi said, "Behold, in the window there is glass, but the glass of the mirror is covered with silver, and no sooner is the silver added then you fail to see others but see only yourself." If you see self and all the respect and honor others ought to give you, you are on dangerous ground. You won't be able to see others if self is in the image you hold in front of you. – Source Unknown

The Bible tells us that God is the Lord Most High. If He is in our hearts as our highest desire, then our life is both blessed and a blessing. There is none greater or higher than He, and therefore there is no greater blessing! Our devotion reflects how high in our hearts He truly is!

BLESSED BY GOD MOST HIGH

Bread & Wine:

Genesis 14:18 ~

Then Melchizedek king of Salem brought out bread and wine. He was priest of God Most High ...

Abram had just fought a tough battle to free some family members and others who really didn't deserve freedom ... he could have justified the bounty he was about to receive financially. Abram was exhausted after the battle; he needed something and someone to help him. Melchizedek, king of Salem, comes to him to minister to him. Melchizedek refreshed Abram and strengthened him. That which we hold "Most High" will be that which "Blesses us Most!" Therefore, the blessing will be only as good as the object offering it! Anything temporal in nature that we hold "most high" is only going to give a temporal blessing: a new car, money or a job. Abram was more interested in the "Bread and Wine" from the Lord's servant than he was for the loot from the King of Sodom! Why? He wasn't as concerned about material things!

Jenny Lind, the great Swedish soprano, disappointed many of her friends because she turned down so many big contracts that would have made her world-famous. One day, a friend surprised her sitting on a sunny sea-shore reading the New Testament. The friend rebuked the singer for not seizing her chances. Quickly, Jenny Lind put her hand over her Testament and said, "I found that making vast sums of money was spoiling my taste for this."

Unlike the King of Sodom, the King of Salem had come to strengthen Abram spiritually and emotionally — not just materially. The King of Salem had come to "commune" with Abram — bread and wine are symbols of communion. Can anything else be higher than God? NO! Therefore, no blessing can be greater than God's!

Blessing Abram:

Genesis 14:19 ~

... and he blessed Abram, saying, "Blessed be Abram by God Most High, Creator of heaven and earth."

What a privilege! "Blessed" is a concept meaning "happy." God can bring true happiness and it will last; material things can't do this! God loves to bless His people with real happiness. It is a personal touch of God that He blessed Abram with, so it is today with us as well. Abram's blessings were coming from the God who created the heavens and the earth – it doesn't get any higher than this! No greater blessing can come from any source higher than the Creator of all things!

BLESSED BE GOD MOST HIGH

Bringer of Victory!

Genesis 14:20a ~

"And praise be to God Most High, who delivered your enemies into your hand."

God deserves for us to bless Him! He has done great things! The victories we experience come from Him. Let's be careful to give Him praise!

A handful of our people went on a mission trip to Eastern Europe several weeks ago. When they came back, they told me they were really impressed with the dedication of the Christians in Rumania. Christians there don't have very much, but they believe they should tithe. They think that's God's standard. But the government of Rumania is repressive, and they are allowed to give only 2.5 percent of their income to charitable organizations. They're trying to minimize the opportunity for any anti-government organization. So Rumanians are searching for loopholes in the law, so that they'll be able to give 10 percent.

The Rumanian Christians have less, and they're looking for a way to give 10 percent. We have more, and we're free to give as we please. In fact, we get a tax break by doing so, and we're looking for loopholes in the Scripture to avoid doing it. What an indictment.

Even in the midst of enemies, we can recognize the privilege of responding to God in giving, for God is the one who gives us victory over our enemies; and He is the one who gives us everything! We should sing, pray, speak about God's greatness, for He is most High! Ultimately, it is God's hand that grants us the victories we experience. God is concerned that we win in battle.

Bounty Given!

Genesis 14:20b ~

Then Abram gave him a tenth of everything.

Notice that Abram not only verbally blessed God but demonstrated it tangibly. Cheerful giver – he gave a tenth of everything he had. Tithes given as an expression of blessing and joy were a way of showing his desire to bless God in more than words! Not tithing because he had to but because he wanted to! So many say tithing was a part of the law ... well, this was before the law! Just like tithing today is after the law! This was one way Abram expressed his blessing to God, and it was an important way. Abram didn't decide to tithe because he thought he HAD to do this, or because it might become a LAW at some point ... his view of material things was such that giving to God was a joy already. His heart was already fixed on God so the "stuff" was not important anyway!

Some say, dedicate the heart and the money will follow; but our Lord put it the other way around. "Where your treasure is, there will your heart be also." If your treasure is dedicated, your heart will be dedicated. If it is not, it simply won't. It is as simple as that.

Abram also did other things as well. He gave a tithe of everything! Not just money. How about giving God your time ... it would be a real blessing to the Lord to have your time occasionally! How about giving God the use of your talents ... it too would bless Him! But giving God these other things are not in place of the tithe, they are in addition to them.

BELONGING TO GOD MOST HIGH

Better Belongings!

Genesis 14:21-23 ~

²¹ The king of Sodom said to Abram, "Give me the people and keep the goods for yourself." ²²But Abram said to the king of Sodom, "With raised hand I have sworn an oath to the Lord, God Most High, Creator of heaven and earth, ²³that I will accept nothing belonging to you, not even a thread or the strap of a sandal, so that you will never be able to say, 'I made Abram rich.'"

The World can only offer us temporal things:
~ Food
~ Money
~ Buildings & things, etc.

God offers us better belongings; He makes us rich:
~ Mercy
~ Love
~ Forgiveness
~ Joy
~ Faith
~ Eternal life!

Whoever or whatever is most high in your mind and heart will determine the kind of belongings you receive!
~ Most high goods
~ Most High God!

Abram didn't even want the world to think it could make him rich! Only God could really do that. God's riches are different than this world's stuff.
~ Abram wasn't saying he didn't need earthly things.
~ He was just saying by refusing the King of Sodom's offer of the world's goods that the things of this world can't make a man truly rich.

This is demonstrated by the fact that he allowed the other men to receive the goods. He was happy with just God! Abram wasn't interested in the wealth of this world; his confidence and trust were in God Himself. I read a quote by Colonel Sanders (of Kentucky Fried Chicken) once that there's no reason to be the richest man in the cemetery.

What would be the point to getting all the wealth of Sodom, anyway? When Abram could have the blessings of God through His servant the King of Salem, why settle for the wealth of Sodom which would soon pass away! As said above by Colonel Sanders ... what's the point to being the richest man in the cemetery!? Better to be wealthy in Heaven!

Belonging to God:

Genesis 14:24 ~

I will accept nothing but what my men have eaten and the share that belongs to the men who went with me—to Aner, Eshkol and Mamre. Let them have their share.

This world cannot offer us anything that will make us truly rich! If the stuff of this world is where we find our happiness, then it is where we find our God! We belong to what we seek! That's why Jesus said, "Seek and ye shall find." What are you seeking for in this life?

My dad borrowed this I'm certain, but he'd say, a tither's problem is seldom money. If our happiness lies in our relationship to God, then we belong to Him and find our happiness in Him. Abram would accept nothing less than belonging to God. Why take something that won't be that valuable in the end like the things of this world, when He could have the God Most High! Abram wasn't opposed to owning things, just opposed to things owning him! His refusal was a refusal to allow the king to think that the goods he offered him would make him rich and happy. Wealth and happiness he already had ... the kind that has no end to it! So, he wouldn't take anything less than the best! God Most High! How about you ... are you willing to settle for something less?

What troubles us most is what we belong to; is it lack of finances, or lack of faith? Is it absence of goods or absence of God? What's most high in your heart will be most high in your devotion. Is God "Jehovah-Elyon" (God Most High) in your heart!?

— 9 —

JEHOVAH-NISSI

The Lord My Banner!

is very fashionable these days to march with a banner waving. Some have marched to the following:

"Ban the Bomb"

"No Nukes"

"Equal Rights"

"Women's Lib"

"Strike"

"Save the Whales" etc.

Everyone marches to some banner, even if it is not written on a placard and held for all to see. All one has to do is look and listen to find out what banner they march to. Our very lives should reflect the very glory of God ... and thus show Him off as our banner.

The Scriptures teach us that as God's people we are to raise high the Lord Jesus as our banner for all men to see! We do this by how we speak and what we reveal in the way we live! The Lord is our banner!

BANNER OF GOD'S AUTHORITY

Attacked!

Exodus 17:8 ~

The Amalekites came and attacked the Israelites at Rephidim.

Forces of this world are opposed to God and His people! Our walk with God will be challenged by this world! The world will challenge our values. The world will challenge our faith in God. The world will challenge our passions and emotions. You cannot live godly and go unchallenged in an ungodly world! Society will challenge your sincerity and faith. Sickness may challenge your trust in God's goodness. Trials will challenge your patience in God's will. A permissive moral atmosphere will challenge your spiritual discipline and God's ideas of right and wrong. Ultimately, however, it won't be the challenges or the damages from the challenges that win, but the testimony despite the challenges that we lift up! Crippled hands raised to God in glory can be a great banner!

Attacking!

Exodus 17:9 ~

Moses said to Joshua, "Choose some of our men and go out to fight the Amalekites. Tomorrow I will stand on top of the hill with the staff of God in my hands."

Standing with the staff of God! Moses' staff was the symbol of God's authority and power. It was a symbol or banner of God's presence and authority! Notice Moses took it to the top of the mountain for all to see! He wanted Israel AND the Amalekites to know that Israel's banner was the Lord's authority, not man's! God's power would prevail as long as the banner of the Lord was held high! Moses held this authority and power in his hands, and so do we today!

The top of the hill was Moses' place of prayer. He often went to the top to pray and be with God. The hill was a symbol of prayer as the source of receiving this authority. It is by prayer that God gives us His authority and power. The disciples learned this with the boy who was an epileptic in Mark 9:14-29. Their authority in trying to cast the sickness out of this boy didn't work. If we don't pray, we won't receive God's power or authority! We dare not stand up against this world or Satan unless we have God's staff in hand!

BANNER OF GOD'S ABILITY

Army!

Exodus 17:10-12 ~

¹⁰So Joshua fought the Amalekites as Moses had ordered, and Moses, Aaron and Hur went to the top of the hill. ¹¹As long as Moses held up his hands, the Israelites were winning, but whenever he lowered his hands, the Amalekites were winning. ¹²When Moses' hands grew tired, they took a stone and put it under him and he sat on it. Aaron and Hur held his hands up—one on one side, one on the other—so that his hands remained steady till sunset.

The effective nature of carrying a banner is determined by having more than one person marching to it! Different responsibilities — one heart of unity! Joshua led the actual fighting. Moses prayed and held up the Lord's staff and gave God's orders. Aaron and Hur supported Moses' weakness, holding his arms as they grew too tired for Moses to keep them up! They all had different jobs to do but one heart to do it, and one banner to march to! By working together, God was able to show Himself strong through His people, and they were able to be victorious! It took their unity for His power to be demonstrated! Their unity was evident by their mutual support, and that support was an indication that God was their banner!

Assurance:

Exodus 17:13 ~

So, Joshua overcame the Amalekite army with the sword.

In prayer and unity there will be victory! You will note that while Moses kept his arms up with the help of Aaron and Hur, it states here that Joshua overcame the enemy with the sword! It was the combined efforts of them all working together under the same banner that allowed them all to win that day! The disciples on the day of Pentecost were "in one accord" and victory came! When Israel built the tabernacle, the leaders had to restrain the people from giving too much! They were united to do something for God and the results were overwhelming – there was power in their sincere unity!

J.B. Phillips said, "God will inevitably appear to disappoint the man who is attempting to use him as a convenience, a prop, or a comfort for his own plans. God has never been known to disappoint the man who sincerely wants to cooperate with his own purposes." Joshua had victory, not because they were just good fighters, but because God was their banner – this assured their victory!

BANNER OF GOD'S ACTIVITY

Announcement!

Exodus 17:14 ~

Then the Lord said to Moses, "Write this on a scroll as something to be remembered and make sure that Joshua hears it, because I will completely blot out the name of Amalek from under heaven."

Memory serves as a reminder that God is our banner. His activity is recorded in our life's story. It is good to remember what God has done; it is like waving the banner of the Lord's goodness. It is a banner we can continue to march to! Moses was told not only to write it down for memory but to be sure Joshua was told about it! This is why we should give testimony to God's goodness. A testimony is like waving a banner.

James S. Hewett shared that, "One Sunday on their way home from church, a little girl turned to her mother and said, 'Mommy, the preacher's sermon this morning confused me.' The mother said, 'Oh? Why is that?' The little girl replied, 'Well, he said that God is bigger than we are. Is that true?' The mother replied, 'Yes, that's true, honey.' 'And he also said that God lives in us? Is that true, Mommy?' Again, the mother replied, 'Yes.' 'Well,' said the little girl, 'if God is bigger than us and He lives in us, wouldn't He show through?'"

It is not enough to write down in our memories the things God has done; they need to be spoken to our brethren! We are to announce that God is our banner and our power!

Altar (Prayer & Praise):

Exodus 17:15-16 ~

[15]*Moses built an altar and called it The Lord is my*

Banner. [16]*He said, "Because hands were lifted up against the throne of the Lord, the Lord will be at war against the Amalekites from generation to generation."*

When we are weak, we have an altar — one of prayer and praise. The altar was a place to bring a sacrifice; here it was a reminder of hands lifted up to the throne of God — of prayer! The very purpose of an altar was to be able to bring a sacrifice. We are called to offer up to God a *"sacrifice of praise."* (Heb. 13:15-16) Praise is another way of waving the banner. It is not as much about an "experience" as much as it is about an "expression" of God as our Banner.

Jesus himself was our sacrifice, "the Lord our Banner!" He said in John 12:32, *"But I, when I am lifted up from the earth, I will draw all men unto myself."*

Which banner are you waving before the world, banners of equal rights, of liberation, of no bombs, or some other temporal thing? These by themselves will never bring a lasting change to the world, only the "Lord our Banner" can do this! In your life, wave before the world the real banner — "Jehovah-Nissi" — THE LORD OUR BANNER! It is a banner you can march to and live by!!

— 10 —

JEHOVAH-RAPHA

The Lord that Heals!

Healing

is a subject of great interest, and sometimes great controversy. Did you know that you are terminally ill! Everyone is going to die! We don't like to admit that truth; we usually reserve that thinking for the one in the hospital dying of cancer!

Men have searched for and proclaimed great cures for sickness and death; i.e., the fountain of youth, a drug that will stop the aging process (now being done in research around the U.S.), and other miracle cures. The trouble is that even with the great strides in medicine, there is much that man cannot cure, even though he has found ways of masking symptoms! And even with man's incredible abilities, there still remain one-cell organisms that can outdo him many times!

Thank God, though, that there is a great physician! He is "Jehovah-Rapha" the "Lord that Heals!" God revealed Himself as one who can heal the most incredible situations, the most horrible of diseases, in both the Old Testament and the New Testament times. And since He never changes, those promises are still good today!

The Bible teaches us that God still heals today in answer to prayer and trust in Him, and that His answer will be the one that we need the most even when it is not always the one we expected!

PAST HEALINGS

Moses & Serpents:

Numbers 21:4-9 ~

⁴They traveled from Mount Hor along the route to the Red Sea, to go around Edom. But the people grew impatient on the way; ⁵they spoke against God and against Moses, and said, "Why have you brought us up out of Egypt to die in the wilderness? There is no bread! There is no water! And we detest this miserable food!"

⁶Then the Lord sent venomous snakes among them; they bit the people and many Israelites died. ⁷The people came to Moses and said, "We sinned when we spoke against the Lord and against you. Pray that the Lord will take the snakes away from us." So, Moses prayed for the people.

⁸The Lord said to Moses, "Make a snake and put it up on a pole; anyone who is bitten can look at it and live." ⁹So Moses made a bronze snake and put it up on a pole. Then when anyone was bitten by a snake and looked at the bronze snake, they lived.

Naaman's Healing:

2 Kings 5:1-14 ~

¹Now Naaman was commander of the army of the king of Aram. He was a great man in the sight of his master and highly regarded, because through him the Lord had given victory to Aram. He was a valiant soldier, but he had leprosy.

²Now bands of raiders from Aram had gone out and had taken captive a young girl from Israel, and she served Naaman's wife. ³She said to her mistress, "If only my master would see the prophet who is in Samaria! He would cure him of his leprosy."

⁴Naaman went to his master and told him what the girl from Israel had said. ⁵"By all means, go," the king of Aram replied. "I will send a letter to the king of Israel." So Naaman left, taking with him ten talents of silver, six thousand shekels of gold and ten sets of clothing. ⁶The letter that he took to the king of Israel read: "With this letter I am sending my servant Naaman to you so that you may cure him of his leprosy."

⁷As soon as the king of Israel read the letter, he tore his robes and said, "Am I God? Can I kill and bring back to life? Why does this fellow send someone to me to be cured of his leprosy? See how he is trying to pick a quarrel with me!"

⁸When Elisha the man of God heard that the king of Israel had torn his robes, he sent him this message: "Why have you torn your robes? Have the man come to me and he will know that there is a prophet in Israel." ⁹So Naaman went with his horses and chariots and stopped at the door of Elisha's house. ¹⁰Elisha sent a messenger to say to him, "Go, wash yourself seven times in the Jordan, and your flesh will be restored and you will be cleansed."

¹¹But Naaman went away angry and said, "I thought that he would surely come out to me and stand and call on the name of the Lord his God, wave his hand over the spot and cure me of my leprosy. ¹²Are not Abana and Pharpar, the rivers of Damascus, better than all the waters of Israel? Couldn't I wash in them and be cleansed?" So he turned and went off in a rage.

¹³Naaman's servants went to him and said, "My father, if the prophet had told you to do some great thing, would you not have done it? How much more, then, when he tells you, 'Wash and be cleansed'!" ¹⁴So he went down and dipped himself in the Jordan seven times, as the man of God had told him, and his flesh was restored and became clean like that of a young boy.

Naaman is an interesting example because he is not even Jewish, though his wife had a Jewish slave that served her. He becomes seriously ill with leprosy or some kind of serious skin disorder the Bible calls leprosy. It was his wife's Jewish slave that tells her that her husband Naaman could find healing through the prophet of God's help … (5:3) *"She said to her mistress, If only my master would see the prophet who is in Samaria! He would cure him of his leprosy."* Naaman, like so many, thought that healing would be accomplished through some mystical or magical means: (5:11) *"But Naaman went away angry and said, 'I thought that he would* surely come out to me and stand and call on the name of the LORD his God, wave his hand over the spot and cure me of my leprosy.'" Naaman expected a wave of the hand and he would be healed! Instead, he had to humble himself and learn obedience to God's Word. When he obeyed however, God wonderfully healed him! (5:14) *"So he went down and dipped himself in the Jordan seven times, as the man of God had told him, and his flesh was restored and became clean like that of a young boy."* His sickness was NOT the result of sin; it was just a part of the general nature of being human.

New Testament Gospels:

Acts 28:7-9 ~

[7] There was an estate nearby that belonged to Publius, the chief official of the island. He welcomed us to his home and showed us generous hospitality for three days. [8] His father was sick in bed, suffering from fever and dysentery. Paul went in to see him and, after prayer, placed his hands on him and healed him. [9] When this had happened, the rest of the sick on the island came and were cured.

The Gospels contain many healings.
~ Lepers were healed.

~ Withered hand was restored.

~ Woman who continuously bled was healed.

~ Peter's mother-in-law was healed.

~ Jairus' daughter was raised from the dead!

~ Blind eyes were opened, deaf ears were restored, lame could again walk, etc., too numerous examples to put here! (28:9) *"When this had happened, the rest of the sick on the island came and were cured."*

PURPOSE IN SUFFERING

Old Testament (Job):

Job's sickness was to teach Job and his friends of God's greatness. Sickness can serve a purpose for a time. It helps us understand the nature of our humanity and the nature of God better. It can also reveal God's glory and power and humble men and reveal our need to trust God.

New Testament:

When we preach the grace of God, healing demonstrates the reality of the Messiah's coming. Healing confirms the Gospel. Healing demonstrates the grace of God and reveals God's glory and power, as in John 9:1-3 (the blind man). It keeps us humble, as in 2 Cor. 12:7 (Paul's thorn in the flesh to keep him from being puffed up!). In Paul's case, it was to keep him humble because of his great revelations. It also kept him depending on God's power, not pride. Suffering can help us understand those who suffer and to identify with others who suffer.

People Who Suffered:

~ Paul in 2 Corinthians 12:7-9 – Thorn was "in his flesh!" (Greek word means physical – as flesh that was around bones.)

~ Paul's illness at Galatia.

Galatians 4:12-16 ~

12I plead with you, brothers and sisters, become like me, for I became like you. You did me no wrong. 13As you know, it was because of an illness that I first preached the gospel to you, 14and even though my illness was a trial to you, you did not treat me with contempt or scorn. Instead, you welcomed me as if I were an angel of God, as if I were Christ Jesus himself. 15Where, then, is your blessing of me now? I can testify that, if you could have done so, you would have torn out your eyes and given them to me. 16Have I now become your enemy by telling you the truth?

~ Trophimus.

2 Timothy 4:20 ~

Erastus stayed in Corinth, and I left Trophimus sick in Miletus.

Trophimus was a companion with Paul on one of his missionary journeys — he became seriously sick. Because of an illness, Paul had to leave Trophimus behind in Miletus. Though many were healed under Paul's ministry, evidently Trophimus here was not. Paul had to leave him behind and continue his ministry without him on this occasion. Why God healed so many others Paul prayed for and not here we don't know.

~ Timothy.

1 Timothy 5:23 ~

Stop drinking only water, and use a little wine because of your stomach and your frequent illnesses.

Timothy was having constant stomach problems. Paul also mentions his OTHER frequent illnesses.

There are many others who suffered physically, though not from illness. It seems ironic that Paul had seen so many healed under his ministry and yet here was his protégé Timothy who evidently struggled with physical issues a lot — without being healed supernaturally. Paul encourages Timothy to use wine medicinally. But this did not dissuade Paul from praying for the sick and seeing many healed supernaturally! This is a mystery why some are healed while others are not, yet the pattern is to pray for the sick that they be healed ... many will be IF we pray! No one will be if we don't! All those healed in the Scripture were healed BECAUSE someone prayed first. Psalm 23:4 says, *"Walk through the valley of shadow of death ... he is with me."* This promise in the Old Testament implies God's presence in the shadow of death, and in the times of sickness and disease.

PURPOSE IN HEALING

Witness to the Gospel:

Mark 16:15-18 ~

[15]He said to them, "Go into all the world and preach the gospel to all creation. [16]Whoever believes and is baptized will be saved, but whoever does not believe will be condemned. [17]And these signs will accompany those

who believe: *In my name they will drive out demons; they will speak in new tongues;* [18]*they will pick up snakes with their hands; and when they drink deadly poison, it will not hurt them at all; they will place their hands on sick people, and they will get well."*

This passage backs up the message that was preached and points to Christ. Healing would be a sign of the Gospel message's truth. This is why missionaries often see such great miracles on the cutting edge of the Gospel. This was true with Jesus ... He was on the cutting edge all the time! Not done for a show or just to make us feel better, healing was done for a purpose. (Jesus refused the demand of the Pharisees to do a miracle for them so they would believe; they only wanted a show, not to believe!)

Signs Follow Believers:

Even here signs follow those who are preaching the Word throughout the world ... signs confirming the message! (16:20) *"Then the disciples went out and preached everywhere, and the Lord worked with them and confirmed his word by the signs that accompanied it."*

These signs are promised not to an individual believer but to the believers as a group. God's people together will see these things happen, not that any one individual alone will have these all happen to him; rather, they are given *"to them."* These signs shall continue until the end!

Witness of God's Grace:

James 5:10-11 ~

[10]Brothers and sisters, as an example of patience in the face of suffering, take the prophets who spoke in the name of the Lord. [11]As you know, we count as blessed those who have persevered. You have heard of Job's perseverance and have seen what the Lord finally brought about. The Lord is full of compassion and mercy.

The symbol of oil is the symbol of God's grace. Grace is given, not demanded or owed. The idea is that in sickness we come to receive, in grace, our healing, but not by demanding it! If demanded, it is no longer grace! It may be that suffering may go on for a time before healing.

Notice the context in James 5:10-11.

1. Patience is a virtue often realized through suffering!
2. Even Job had to be patient, but God did heal him

later!

3. Keep praying ... though it has been some time you have suffered, God's grace will come (5:11). God has some reason for it that will make you a better Christian in the end!

Sometimes healing comes delayed rather than immediately. What is significant here is that James says when you are sick to CALL for the elders of the church to pray over you! There is healing available. The prayer of faith can bring healing. It is possible. This would not be a biblical text if it weren't available! There would be no sense of doing this if healing weren't possible! The text mentions BOTH forgiveness and healing are possible!

Why has this been so ignored by the church today when God has made it available? Most of the time we ignore it because we are uncomfortable worrying about the possibility of someone NOT being healed. Well, no one will be healed if we don't pray in faith, for *"without faith it is impossible to please God"* ... and by praying in faith someone just might be healed! Wouldn't that be wonderful? Maybe we should worry about what will happen if someone DOES get healed!

PROGRAM FOR HEALING

Prayer & Faith:

James 5:14-16 ~

¹⁴Is anyone among you sick? Let them call the elders of the church to pray over them and anoint them with oil in the name of the Lord. ¹⁵And the prayer offered in faith will make the sick person well; the Lord will raise them up. If they have sinned, they will be forgiven. ¹⁶Therefore confess your sins to each other and pray for each other so that you may be healed. The prayer of a righteous person is powerful and effective.

Pray believing God's best will be done! To pray means to ask specifically what you need. Faith means to trust that God will give you what you need! (Even if the answer is different than what you thought you needed, it will be what you need most!)

Seek God First!

2 Chronicles 16:12 ~

In the thirty-ninth year of his reign Asa was afflicted with a disease in his feet. Though his disease was severe, even in his illness he did not seek help from the Lord, but only from the physicians.

Asa sought help ONLY (NIV) from the physicians.

Idea: It is not wrong to go to a doctor, but go to the great Physician first! Your prayer of faith will cause the sick person to hear from God, and God will raise him up! Sometimes it is immediate. Sometimes it is later. Ultimately, all of us will be healed of the ultimate illness (death); we will be resurrected! Some who have followed the Scriptures here and have not been healed shouldn't necessarily feel guilty, or that it is their fault; it may be God hasn't yet finished His purpose in our suffering. No matter when, we should always pray for healing, believing God will heal, and then allow God to be God and to trust in Him!

Thanksgiving & Trust:

I Peter 4:19 ~

So then, those who suffer according to God's will should commit themselves to their faithful Creator and continue to do good.

Trust God when you don't understand! Be thankful even in suffering, knowing this, that the trial of your faith will work patience, and when patience has had her perfect work, we will be mature! (James 1:2-4) God's greatest healing is perfecting us into the image of His son! It is like gold going through fire. The fire purifies gold making it more valuable and usable. Physical sickness may bring spiritual healing and not just physical healing! (I Pet. 4:1-2)

I recently read a story by a woman who said that as a girl she was poor. She said, "I grew up in a cold water flat, but I married a man who had money. And he took me up to a place where I had flowers, and I had gardens, and I had grass. It was wonderful. And we had children.

"Then suddenly I became physically sick. I went to the hospital, and the doctors ran all sorts of tests. One night the doctor came into my room, and with a long look on his face, said, 'I'm sorry to tell you this. Your liver has stopped working.'

"I said, 'Doctor, wait a minute. Wait a minute. Are you telling me that I am dying?' And he said, 'I, I can't tell you any more than that. Your liver has stopped working. We've done everything we can to start it.' And he walked out.

"I knew I was dying. I was so weak; I had to feel my way along the corridor down to the chapel of the hospital. I wanted to tell God off. I wanted to tell God, 'You are a shyster! You've been passing yourself off as a loving God for two thousand years, but every time anyone begins to get happy you pull the rug out from under them.' I wanted this to be a face-to-face telling off of God.

"And just as I got into the center aisle of the chapel, I tripped, I swooned, and I fainted. And I looked up, and there stenciled along the step into the sanctuary, where the altar is, I saw these words: LORD, BE MERCIFUL TO ME A SINNER. I know God spoke to me that night. I know he did."

She didn't say how God communicated this to her, but what God said was, "You know what this is all about. It's about the moment of surrender; it's about bringing you to that moment when you will surrender everything to me. These doctors, they do the best they can, but they only treat. I'm the only one who can cure you."

And she said, "There with my head down on my folded arms in the center of the chapel, repeating, 'Lord, be merciful to me a sinner,' I surrendered to God. I found my way back to my hospital bed, weak as I was.

"The next morning, after the doctor ran the blood tests and the urinalysis and so forth, he said, 'Your liver has started working again. We don't know why. We don't know why it stopped, and we don't know why it started up again.' And I said in my heart, but I know. Oh, but I know. God has brought me to the brink of disaster, just to get me to turn my life over to him." – John Powell, "Prayer as Surrender," Preaching Today, Tape No. 108.

The most important healing we can realize is not just the physical! Too often we limit healing to the physical realm which is only a temporal thing. What greater healing than for God, through sickness, to bring about an eternal healing spiritually! Physical healing is always temporary ... it is still *"appointed unto man once to die and after that to face judgment!"* (Heb. 9:27) Spiritual healing, however, has an eternal quality to it! Even if our bodies continue to decay, our destination is eternity with God! In fact, physical healing is a testimony of the fact that if God can heal us physically, He can also heal us spiritually!

Remember the man for whom Jesus forgave his sins; upon being questioned about it, He healed the man to demonstrate that forgiving sins was greater, and if He can do that, He can do the lesser. (Mark 2:1-12)

God still heals today! Sometimes it is physical. Sometimes it is spiritual. Sometimes it is both! However, His power and love are the same! Don't be afraid to come to Him for healing, for He is still "JEHOVAH-

RAPHA" the "Lord that Heals!"

God is a God of healing! There are many kinds of healing. He asks that we ask Him for our healing and then trust in Him to heal in the time and way that will be for our best interest. He will heal us because He is "JEHOVAH-RAPHA" the "Lord that Heals!"

About the Author

Reverend Tim R. Barker is the Superintendent of the South Texas District of the Assemblies of God which is headquartered in Houston, Texas.

He is a graduate of Southwestern Assemblies of God University, with a Bachelor of Science degree in General Ministries/Biblical Studies, with a minor in music. He also received a Master of Arts in Practical Theology from SAGU and received his Doctorate of Ministry Degree from West Coast Seminary.

Reverend Barker was ordained by the Assemblies of God in 1989. He began his ministry in the South Texas District in 1984 as youth & music minister and continued his ministry as Pastor, Executive Presbyter (2006 – 2009) and Executive Secretary-Treasurer (2009 – 2011) in the South Texas District, where he served until his election as the South Texas District Superintendent in 2011.

By virtue of his district office, Reverend Barker is a member of the District's Executive Presbytery and the General Presbytery of the General Council of the Assemblies of God, Springfield, Missouri. He is a member of the Executive Board of Regents for Southwestern Assemblies of God University, Waxahachie, Texas and SAGU-American Indian College, Phoenix, Arizona. He is a member of the Board of Directors of Pleasant Hills Children's Home, Fairfield, Texas, as well as numerous other boards and committees.

Reverend Barker and his wife, Jill, married in 1983, have been blessed with two daughters. Jordin and her husband, Stancle Williams, who serves as the South Texas District Youth Director. Abrielle and her husband, Nolan McLaughlin, are church planters of Motion Church in San Antonio. The Barkers have four grandchildren, Braylen, Emory and Landon Williams and Kingston McLaughlin.

His unique style of pulpit ministry and musical background challenges the body of Christ, with an appeal that reaches the generations.

Contact Tim

Pastor Tim would love to hear from you. You can reach him at www.TimBarker.ag.

Click on Ask Pastor Tim for more information